'I loved this book! Ros paints com  women and shows how they are fa victims. Though the reflections are practical, illustrating the beauty of Go........................., messy world.'
Sarah Allen, Course Director, Flourish North

'The Old Testament meets everyday life in these forty stories of envy, grief, shame, courage, faith and hope, from famous women in the Bible's limelight to anonymous bit players. Not just for women! Culminating with New Testament stories, Ros Clarke's gritty devotions will pack a punch for anyone seeking to deepen reflection and prayer in Lent or at any other time.'
The Revd Dr Jill Firth, Lecturer in Hebrew and Old Testament, Ridley College, Melbourne

'In these devotions, Dr Clarke explores the minds and emotions of forty biblical women from Eve to Mary Magdalene. She skilfully uses the concerns of the contemporary reader to try to understand something of the experiences of the women and concludes with questions for thought and prayer. She does not hide the women's faults as she depicts their struggles and achievements, but gives them the voice of praise and thanks as a challenge to us.'
Peter Jensen, former Archbishop of Sydney and General Secretary of GAFCON

'In this compelling and enriching survey, Dr Clarke is faithful to Scripture and to the humanity of the women it presents. I found myself moved to laughter and tears, inspired by courage and resilience – in short, confronted with the reality of the human heart before God, and his holiness, faithfulness and steadfast love to his own. Men and women in the church have so much to learn and pray

about when it comes to our flourishing together; this book will help them considerably with that.'
Niv Lobo, curate, Highfield Church, Southampton

'This book will flood your heart with the truth of God's mercy passionately pursuing the hearts of women: the hearts of his beloved daughters. By looking at the lives of real women in all the mess and depravity caused by them and inflicted on them, Dr Clarke points us to the gracious, powerful, redemptive work of God.

'Not shying away from the reality of sin that grips our hearts, from the shame and despair that threaten our thought lives, body image and speech, Dr Clarke leads us to look to Christ alone for our redemption and refuge. As we lift our hearts to him, using Dr Clarke's pertinent prayers at the end of each devotion, steeped in faithful, powerful exposition of Scripture, our hearts' hope is rooted in Christ alone.'
Emily Lucas, MTh student, Union School of Theology

'Fresh, honest, faithful and perceptive. These devotions bring together a striking turn of phrase, a keen eye for what many may miss or hide in the text, and a personal and pastoral heart that is unafraid to broach subjects that are too often neglected. Highly recommended!'
James Robson, Ministry Director, Keswick Ministries

'This is good reading for women, young and old, *and* for men, both young and old. Each story is beautifully told, and in each case the connection is opened up for life for women and men today in our schools, homes and everywhere. Each person is honoured and each circumstance is seen from the perspective of both the woman and the God who loves her.

'May God make us men and women who do not accept that sin is normalized, but who know the way of being saved, through God's coming, born of a woman! May this book help us, as we read of our sisters in Scripture, to become the women and men God made us to be.'

Bishop Keith Sinclair, National Director, Church of England Evangelical Council

FORTY WOMEN

Ros Clarke is Associate Director of Church Society, a fellowship that contends to reform and renew the Church of England in biblical faith. Ros lived and studied in Oxford, London, Philadelphia and the Scottish Highlands before returning to settle in her home town of Stafford. She has a PhD on the Song of Songs, and is an experienced writer and speaker who is particularly passionate about training and equipping women for ministry. In 2018, she established the Priscilla Programme, an online training course for women who serve in volunteer ministries.

FORTY WOMEN

Unseen women
of the Bible from
Eden to Easter

Ros Clarke

INTER-VARSITY PRESS
36 Causton Street, London SW1P 4ST, England
Email: ivp@ivpbooks.com
Website: www.ivpbooks.com

First published 2021
Reprinted 2022

British Library Cataloguing-in-Publication Data
A catalogue record for this book is available from the British Library.

ISBN: 978-1-78974-356-2
eBook ISBN: 978-1-78974-357-9

Set in Minion Pro 10.25/13.75pt
Typeset in Great Britain by CRB Associates, Potterhanworth, Lincolnshire
Printed and bound in Great Britain by Clays Ltd, Elcograf S.p.A.

Produced on paper from sustainable sources

*Inter-Varsity Press publishes Christian books that are true to the Bible and that
communicate the gospel, develop discipleship and strengthen the church for its mission
in the world.*

*IVP originated within the Inter-Varsity Fellowship, now the Universities and Colleges
Christian Fellowship, a student movement connecting Christian Unions in universities and
colleges throughout Great Britain, and a member movement of the International Fellowship
of Evangelical Students. Website: www.uccf.org.uk. That historic association is maintained,
and all senior IVP staff and committee members subscribe to the UCCF Basis of Faith.*

For all the women whose stories have not been told and
whose voices have not been heard

Contents

Contents

Foreword

Jesus' treatment of women was revolutionary. He welcomed and commended women others overlooked and scorned. Bleeding women. Poor women. Physically disabled women. Notoriously sinful women. Single women. Older women. Foreign women. Prostitutes. Jesus saw and loved women as beings made in the image of God. But while Jesus saw women in utterly extraordinary ways, this was not the first time in the Bible that women were seen.

The first person in the Bible to name God was Hagar, who 'called the name of the LORD who spoke to her, "You are a God of seeing"' (Genesis 16:13, ESV). God saw Hagar and protected her. But Hagar is also an early scriptural example of a woman being mistreated. Her story is a story of enslavement, of being presented for sex and surrogacy to her master by her mistress, and then of being so badly treated by her mistress, Sarah, that she fled and would have died if God had not met with her and made her unbelievable promises.

In this book, Ros Clarke helps *us* to see the women of the Bible with fresh eyes. She walks us through a full spectrum of stories – from Queen Esther to Queen Jezebel, and from the God-fearing Canaanite Rahab to the God-fearing Moabite Ruth – and invites us to full-orbed vision of each woman she presents.

An expert in the Song of Songs, Dr Clarke draws our gaze towards Old Testament women, both named and anonymous, leading us into their stories and their struggles and giving us space to connect them with our own. As I read through this book, I found myself seeing elements I'd missed and being wooed to the Scriptures in fresh ways.

While the book majors on Old Testament narratives, Dr Clarke helps us to see the ways in which the Hebrew Scriptures point us to Jesus as they present these women, and she ends with a handful of

New Testament women who encountered the longed-for Christ for themselves.

In John's gospel, the risen Jesus first reveals himself by saying a woman's name: 'Mary' (John 20:16). He is the one who sees and knows us best. He is the one who calls us each by name. As you work through this book, my hope and prayer is that you'll hear his call afresh each day.

Rebecca McLaughlin
Founder of Vocable Communications
and author of *Confronting Christianity and the Secular Creed*

Acknowledgments

This book would not have been written without the inspiration of my dear friend, Emily Hubbard, who announced on Shrove Tuesday in 2019 on Twitter that she was embarking on a Lenten writing project. Thanks, Emily, for letting me borrow your idea, which ultimately ended up becoming this book!

Very great thanks also to my boss, Lee Gatiss, and my employers at Church Society, for encouraging me in this project and giving me time to work on it.

Finally, thanks to my editor, Tom Creedy, who read my blogposts and got in touch to say he thought there might be a book in them. Thank you so much for championing this project and making it a reality, Tom.

Acknowledgements

Introduction

I had not made any specific plans for a Lenten discipline in 2019. My preference is usually to take up a particular practice rather than to give something up. And so when one of my Twitter friends announced on Shrove Tuesday that she was embarking on a Lenten writing project, the idea appealed to me greatly. As I mulled it over that evening, I wondered if I could write about some of the unsung women in the Old Testament each day during Lent. I began to scribble down the names and stories which came to mind, in order to check that I had enough. The list grew. And grew. And became more diverse and more intriguing.

So, I began on Ash Wednesday with a blogpost about Eve. And every day, I looked forward to the time in the evening when I would think about the next woman, or the next group of women. Their stories were all different, and yet there were some obvious themes emerging: women who struggled with infertility; women who protected children; women who were abused; women who were overlooked; women who were faithful in the most desperate circumstances; and women who were wicked beyond belief.

What I hadn't expected was to find so much contemporary resonance with their stories. There are women here who would have been at the forefront of the #MeToo movement. There are women who can teach us about body image, beauty and shame. There are women whose intensely personal stories of grief and love transcend cultural differences.

Many of these women are not the heroines of their own stories, in the way that the Bible tells them. Many of them are often-forgotten side notes in the stories of men and nations. Some of these women are among the many anonymous characters in the narrative of the

Bible. But they are there. They are there because God wants us to know about them. Because their stories do have something to say to us about being God's people. Because these women play their part in salvation history. Because they too are made in God's image.

In this book, I turn the spotlight on these women. Some of them you will know very well, but others you may never have noticed previously. We're told a lot about some of them and so I have selected specific incidents to consider. We're told very little about others and I have tried to deduce from the scant information something of their stories. In every case, I have been conscious of the need to remember that these were real people, not merely one-dimensional ciphers. Women, as much as men, are complex people, capable of great good and great evil. They may have deep faith and yet succumb to moments of temptation. The stories are not allegorical morality tales but real lives lived out in a world as messy and complicated as our own.

That's why, incidentally, although this is a book *about* women, it is not a book only *for* women. These women are not part of the Bible's story in order to show women how to be women, any more than the men are there simply to teach men how to be men. The Bible is God's word for all God's people. And that is really my point: women are people too. If you want to learn how to trust God when your world is ending, consider the widow of Zarephath. If you want an example of someone giving everything they hold dear to the Lord, remember Hannah. If you want to explore the depths of human depravity, Jezebel and Athaliah will show you. If you are looking for models of biblical leadership, read about Deborah, or of courageously destroying the Lord's enemy, consider Jael.

On which note, I should point out that this book is not what you might call 'family-friendly'. It does not shy away from the violence, the abuse, the sexual assault and rape that the biblical narratives describe and allude to. These are not women whose lives were spent in needlework and prayer. These women lived in the dark realities of the broken, sinful world and many of them experienced it at its very worst. Let's not dishonour them by sugar-coating their stories but respect them by hearing their voices, even when that makes for uncomfortable reading.

There are forty chapters in this book, although they include slightly more than forty women because some are considered in pairs or small groups. If you follow Lent from Ash Wednesday to Maundy Thursday, remembering that Sundays are not included, you will have a chapter for each day. There is a suggested Bible reading as well as the key verse for the chapter. At the end of each chapter, there are a couple of questions for you to consider and a prayer that you could use in response to what you've read.

As I reworked, rewrote and added to the original blogposts that became this book, some of the women from the New Testament were included alongside those from the Old. And so the book ends, appropriately, on the first Easter Sunday, with a woman meeting her risen Lord in a garden.

It is my prayer that, as you spend time with each of these women, you too will seek Christ and cling to him, and that you will find him and be transformed by him.

Ros Clarke
Stafford

1

Eve

Adam and his wife were both naked, and they felt no shame.
(Genesis 2:25)

Bible reading: Genesis 2:18–25

We begin, of course, with Eve. Eve was a woman unlike any other because she alone among women knew what it was to live in a world without sin. She walked and worked in a garden-world without weeds or thistles. She loved and lived in a marriage without sin. Nothing had been spoiled. Not yet. Nothing had been broken or twisted, bent or withered under the curse. There was true freedom to enjoy all God's good creation. There was only one rule, and that was a good one, for their protection and blessing.

I can barely even begin to imagine what that was like. No disappointment, no frustration, no despair and no misery. Joy and delight in their marriage; satisfaction and fulfilment in their work. Freedom from fear, freedom from pain and freedom from shame.

That's what it says at the end of Genesis 2, before everything began to go wrong: 'Adam and his wife were both naked, and they felt no shame' (Genesis 2:25).

It's a strange comment, isn't it? Why would we think there might be any shame when there was no sin to be ashamed of?

But the writer knows that shame is more complicated than that.

Shame doesn't have to be earned. It doesn't have to be deserved. Shame is not always the result of our own shameful acts.

Shame can be pressed upon us for all kinds of reasons. Our bodily functions and appearance are an easy vehicle for others to make us feel ashamed. Readers of Genesis might well have experienced

1

nakedness as something shameful, but Adam and his wife Eve did not.

Not yet.

Women are shamed for their bodies in all kinds of ways: shamed for having breasts that are too large or breasts that are too small; shamed for being too curvy or too straight; shamed for having periods and for not having periods; shamed for infertility; and shamed for having bodies that have been reshaped by pregnancy. We are shamed for our sexuality: for enjoying sex or for being frigid; for 'playing hard to get'; and for 'asking for it'. We are even shamed for being the victims of sexual assault.

From a frighteningly early age, girls learn to be ashamed of their bodies, ashamed of their femaleness and ashamed of their sexuality.

But Eve was naked with her husband and felt no shame.

When we teach girls that their bodies are not shameful, when teenagers learn that they don't have to be embarrassed to go through puberty, and when women can be naked with their husbands and feel no shame in it, then we give them the opportunity to experience a little glimpse of Eve's paradise.

The gospel promise is that, one day, we will once again walk face to face with our heavenly bridegroom in the true paradise – a world that is once again without sin – and then we too will know what it is like to be free from fear, free from pain and free from shame.

For reflection

- Is your body, male or female, a source of shame for you? Where has this shame come from?
- How could you help children or teenagers you know to grow up without such shame?

Prayer

Creator God,
who made Adam and Eve without sin and without shame,

teach us not to be ashamed of our bodies.
We praise you that your Son, our Saviour Jesus Christ,
was not ashamed to take on human flesh
nor to endure the cross, scorning its shame on our behalf.
Though the world is now full of pain, fear and shame,
thank you that, because of him,
we can have the confidence and joy of Eve.
Amen.

2

Sarai

[Sarai] said to Abram, 'The LORD has kept me from having children. Go, sleep with my slave; perhaps I can build a family through her.'

(Genesis 16:2)

Bible reading: Genesis 16:1–6

The Old Testament is a book about infertility.

Beginning with Sarai and ending with Elizabeth (whose story may be told in the New Testament but, nonetheless, marks the end of the old covenant era), woman after woman fails to get pregnant. It's all the more pointed and poignant because of the many women whose sole function in the narrative is to marry and have children. Mothers are ten a penny in the Old Testament. But the women we know, the women we remember, the women whose stories matter, those women are, all too often, barren.

And so it is with Sarai, the exceptionally beautiful wife of Abram. She's followed her husband all the way from Haran into the land of Canaan. She's gone down with him into Egypt to avoid the famine and, while they were there, she even agreed to his ridiculous plan to pretend she was his sister so that he wouldn't be killed by Pharaoh. She's gone back with him to Canaan and settled in Hebron. Through all that time, she's remembered what God promised her husband: that his descendants would become a great nation. Maybe she'd wondered, after all that time, whether God was ever going to keep his promise. Abram did. He worried that he had no children, but then God reiterated the promise: Abram would have an heir of his own flesh and blood and descendants more numerous than the stars in the sky.

What's a woman to do when her husband is supposed to be fathering a vast nation of descendants and she can't get pregnant?

She says to her husband, 'The LORD has kept me from having children. Go, sleep with my slave; perhaps I can build a family through her' (Genesis 16:2).

This enslaved woman is to be no more than a surrogate. Her child will not be for herself. Her child will be a means for Sarai to build a family. Because, after all, God has promised that it would be only Abram's flesh and blood, not Sarai's. And since she can't have a child of her own, she'll have to take the child of her slave and make him her own.

She's resourceful.

She's desperate.

And she's cruel.

Because Hagar does sleep with Abram. She does get pregnant. And she does, as a result, begin to look down on her mistress. The shame of infertility, you see.

But Sarai isn't taking that; not from her slave. She whines to her husband, complaining that he's done exactly what she wanted him to. And then she's cruel. So cruel that Hagar, pregnant Hagar, a slave with nothing of her own and no man to protect her, prefers to run away rather than stay another day in Sarai's household.

Infertility is a curse. When God tells Eve that he will multiply her pain in childbearing, he doesn't just mean the pain of labour. Everything connected with childbearing is painful and difficult. Menstruation is painful and difficult. Pregnancy is painful and difficult. Labour is painful and difficult. Miscarriage is painful and difficult. Menopause is painful and difficult.

Infertility is painful and difficult.

Infertility makes Sarai desperate and destructive. She jeopardizes her marriage, forces another woman into having sex with her husband and then drives her, vulnerable and alone, out of the household and into the wilderness.

And at the end of it all, Sarai is still childless. Because in the story that the Bible is telling about infertility, human intervention isn't the answer. This isn't a story about surrogacy, about IVF or even about adoption, though some of those may be appropriate ways to respond to infertility now. The Bible is telling a different story, in which infertility is the setting for divine intervention.

Again and again, you see, the barren woman in the Bible gives birth. The old woman, the overlooked woman or the first wife who may be loved but isn't blessed. The woman whose hope has long since died, even though her faith remains. The Lord makes his face to shine upon that woman and is gracious to her.

Sarai's actions are disgraceful. God's response is grace.

Not only grace to give her a child later. But grace to turn her desperation into true faith. Grace to turn her manipulation and cruelty into gentle obedience. Grace that transforms Sarai into Sarah.

For reflection

- When have you experienced desperation like Sarah's? How did it make you behave?
- Where in your life do you need God's grace to transform your disgrace?

Prayer

Almighty God,
who alone can transform desperation into true faith,
depravity into holiness,
self-gratification into obedience
and despair into hope,
we turn to you today, in our shame and disgrace.
By your grace, transform us by the power of the gospel,
so that we may live in faith and obedience,
in holiness and hope,

showing kindness to others no matter how desperate our own
circumstances.
Amen.

3

Hagar

She gave this name to the LORD who spoke to her: 'You are the God who sees me,' for she said, 'I have now seen the One who sees me.'
(Genesis 16:13)

Bible reading: Genesis 16:7–14

It's no fun being an invisible woman. A woman who gets to play only a bit part in the story of someone else's life.

If you're an invisible woman, no one listens to you. No one sees you. No one's interested in what you want, what you think or how you feel. Hagar was an invisible woman.

No one asks Hagar whether she wants to sleep with Abram. No one asks whether she wants to have his baby. No one asks whether she's fine with handing that baby over to another woman. Hagar doesn't matter. It's only her body, her baby, her life after all.

But when Sarai adds insult to injury, treating Hagar cruelly for following her own orders, finally she snaps. This is Hagar's life and it's time for her to take control of it. So she runs away. Sarai and Abram don't come after her. But there is someone who sees what's happening and who knows how miserable she is. Someone who cares.

An angel of the Lord meets Hagar. He tells her that she will have to return and submit. But he also makes her a promise. Her descendants, just like Abram's, will be too numerous to count. Hagar's son won't be forgotten. Her son won't be nothing. He will not be invisible, overlooked or worthless, as his mother has been. Ishmael's very name, 'God hears', will be a daily reminder that God heard Hagar's misery. He will be a blessing but he won't be easy, she's told. He will be a wild donkey of a man, continually in conflict.

Hagar's life is transformed by this encounter. It's not just the promises about her baby. It's something far more profound. For the first time, the invisible woman has been seen.

'She gave this name to the LORD who spoke to her: "You are the God who sees me," for she said, "I have now seen the One who sees me"' (Genesis 16:13).

God sees Hagar. She isn't invisible to him. Her story matters to him. He listens. He cares.

God sees you. You aren't invisible to him. You aren't overlooked by him. You aren't worthless to him. Your story matters to him. He sees. He listens. He cares.

There's no happy ending to Hagar's story. She still has to go back to Sarai and her cruel taunts. She still has to give birth to Ishmael, knowing he's going to be hard, hard work.

But she's not invisible any more. She's been seen. She can hold her head up high. She has seen the one who sees her.

In God's eyes, there are no bit-part actors. There are no invisible women. You matter. He cares. He sees.

For reflection

- Do you ever feel as if you have only a bit-part in someone else's story? Do you think other people might feel like that about you?
- What difference does it make to know that God sees you and knows you, and that he values those people you don't even notice or care about?

Prayer

O God who sees us,
who knows us in our inmost being,
who values and cares for us in every way,
you know the people we have overlooked;

you value and care for the people we have counted worthless.
Transform the way we see ourselves
and teach us to see others as you see them.
Amen.

4

Rebekah

'My son, let the curse fall on me.'
(Genesis 27:13)

Bible reading: Genesis 27:1–13

Mothers don't have favourite children. They'll all tell you that. 'No, no. Of course I love them all equally,' they'll say. And sometimes it's true.

But sometimes mothers do have favourite children. Sometimes it's the easy child; the smiling, obedient, sleeping child. Sometimes it's the wild child; the fun, unpredictable, never-a-dull-moment child. Sometimes it's the child who is just like her father or the child who breaks every mould.

How does that feel, having a favourite child? Having to hide the favouritism all the time and pretend, 'No, no. I love them all equally.' How does it feel when those children aren't even born yet? When they're still growing inside their mother's womb and she can feel them fighting each other? She knows that's not normal, and when she asks God about it, he tells her, 'Two nations are in your womb, and two peoples from within you will be separated; one people will be stronger than the other, and the elder will serve the younger' (Genesis 25:23).

Who can blame Rebekah for having a favourite son? Even God, it seems, prefers her younger boy over her elder. Jacob is the golden boy, the favoured son. Only Isaac has a soft spot for Esau. But Isaac is old. Isaac can be fooled.

Mothers will do anything for their children. Lay down their own lives for them, even. And Rebekah is no exception. She sees a chance to grab hold of a blessing for Jacob. Not just any blessing. *The* blessing. The blessing of being his father's heir; the heir to the promises made to his grandfather, Abraham.

She wants history to record that God is the God of Abraham, Isaac and Jacob, not Abraham, Isaac and Esau. She'll do whatever it takes and so she says, 'My son, let the curse fall on me' (Genesis 27:13).

Jacob will be blessed and Rebekah will take the curse. She'll deserve it, of course.

She has lied and deceived, and manipulated and schemed. She's shown favouritism to one son over the other. She's done whatever it takes. She is not an innocent victim of the curse.

She's done whatever it takes. And in so doing, she has made the prophecy come true.

I wonder if Rebekah ever came to realize that the end did not justify the means. That God would have found a way to realize his prophecy without her sinful intervention. That we can trust him with the future, we can trust him with our loved ones and we can trust him with our children.

We can seek their blessing without sacrificing our own.

We can love one child without hating the other.

For reflection

- Do you find it hard to trust that God will fulfil his promises without having to compromise on your principles?
- The New Testament defines love as laying down one's life for another person (see John 15:13 and 1 John 3:16). Are there limits to what this self-sacrifice should entail?

Prayer

Loving Father,
whose own Son came that our curse might fall on him,
teach us to follow his example of sacrificial love.

Rebekah

But guard us from the pride and lack of faith
that caused Rebekah to sacrifice herself by sinning.
May we always put our trust in you,
knowing that our faithful obedience
will never frustrate your good purposes.
Amen.

5

Rachel

'I have had a great struggle with my sister, and I have won.'
(Genesis 30:8)

Bible reading: Genesis 29:31–35; Genesis 30:1–8

You'd think it would be the plain sister whose life was twisted and
bitter with jealousy and envy. But no. In this case, it turns out that
it's the pretty one. It's the pretty one who had to wait for seven years
to be married to her beloved Jacob. It's the pretty one who had to
watch her sister produce child after child, son after son, while she
herself remained childless. It's Rachel who is the one eaten up with
envy, not Leah.

It's never hard to find a reason to be envious. There's always a filter
that makes another person's grass look greener. They're richer than
you, more popular or wiser; they have a better job, a better home or
a better marriage; they aren't living with chronic illness or disability;
they haven't suffered great tragedy. They have what you want.

We can always find a reason to be envious because we can always
find something else to want. For Rachel, it was simple: she wanted
what Leah had. She won't be the only sibling to have experienced that
kind of envy. She certainly wasn't the only wife in a polygamous
marriage to have experienced it. There are a number of instances of
polygamy in the Old Testament, and it's never explicitly prohibited
in Old Testament laws. But it never works out well for those who
ignore the prototype of marriage shown in Genesis 2, in which one
man and one woman establish their new family.

It doesn't work out well for Rachel. She wanted what her sister had:
she wanted a son. Rachel was married to Jacob just a week later than

her elder sister, but while Leah had given birth to Reuben, to Simeon, to Levi and to Judah, Rachel remained childless.

She demands a son in dramatic fashion, saying to Jacob, 'Give me children, or I'll die!' (Genesis 30:1). The desperation of the infertile woman is, as we've already seen, deeply embedded in the Bible's story. But for Rachel here, the desperation is not about the child she longs for so much as it is about the sister she envies.

Jacob makes the mistake of husbands everywhere, replying to an emotional outburst with logic: 'Am I in the place of God, who has kept you from having children?' (Genesis 30:2). It's not his fault and he's angry that she is accusing him. Obviously it's not his fault, since he has plenty of children with Leah. And, presumably, since he loves Rachel so much, he's been having sex with her more often than with her sister. What's he to do about it?

So Rachel does what Sarai did: she sends her servant Bilhah in, to build her family that way. Bilhah does indeed bear two sons and, for Rachel, this is a triumph. It's not a triumph over her infertility nor a triumph over Jacob or God. No, for Rachel, it's all about one person: 'I have had a great struggle with my sister, and I have won' (Genesis 30:8).

Winning and losing. There is no joy in the children for themselves, just as Rachel seems to have taken no joy in her many nephews. For Rachel, it was all about triumphing over her elder, plainer, less-beloved sister.

But her triumph doesn't last long. Leah does exactly the same as Rachel. She sends her servant in to Jacob, and she too bears a child. And another. So now Leah has children of her own and the children of her servant, while Rachel has children only by her servant. She got what she wanted but now she wants more. Her discontent isn't satisfied by the arrival of Bilhah's sons. Instead, her discontent breeds only further discontent.

Leah, having thought her childbearing years were over, goes on to have two more sons and a daughter.

Rachel, having thought she'd finally won against her sister, goes on to become more and more envious.

Eventually, God does relent, giving Rachel a son. Is she satisfied, finally?

'She named him Joseph, and said, "May the LORD add to me another son"' (Genesis 30:24).

The truth that Rachel never learns is that there is only one way to be satisfied, and it is not by getting the things that you want. That only makes you want more. There is only one secret to being content in every situation, whether you are in need or have enough, whether well fed or hungry, whether living in plenty or in want. The secret, as Paul discovered thousands of years later, is not to try to find our contentment in our circumstances. The secret is to find contentment in our Saviour (see Philippians 4:12).

For reflection

- Why is envy such a self-destructive emotion? How did it affect Rachel?
- Whose life do you envy? Do you think you would be satisfied if you were to have what those you envy have?

Prayer

Lord God,
forgive me for those times when I have looked with envy on others,
when I have longed for the blessings they enjoy
and when I have failed to rejoice in their happiness.
Protect me from the envy that destroys families,
spoils friendships
and is never satisfied.
Teach me to find true contentment in the Lord, my Saviour,
in whom are found all blessings and who satisfies all desires.
In his name I pray.
Amen.

6

Leah

Then Leah said, 'How happy I am! The women will call me happy.'
(Genesis 30:13)

Bible reading: Genesis 29:16–30; Genesis 30:9–13

It's hard not to compare yourself with other people. They say it's particularly hard for women, but I don't know. I think it's hard for all of us. Especially when the comparison is obvious to everyone. When it's visible at first glance. When Rachel is the beautiful sister and Leah is the plain one.

One look at the beautiful sister, the pretty woman whom everyone has always loved, and Jacob is smitten. Of course he is. So smitten that he'll do anything for her. Work seven years? No problem! Work seven more? It'll be his pleasure.

Jacob does not even notice the other sister. The older sister: the one whose eyes aren't sparkling and whose hair doesn't fall into pretty waves, and who isn't petite in the right places and curvy in the other right places. But her father notices. Her father notices that all through those seven years while Jacob has been labouring to win Rachel, no other man has come to ask for Leah. No one has seen past her plain outward appearance. No one has thought that perhaps, even though her younger sister is spoken for, Leah might still be worth having.

Laban notices and so he plans. And when he tells Leah his audacious plan, I expect she might have felt a moment of triumph. A little thrill that, just for once, she is going to get the thing her little sister wants and not the other way round. Leah would be Jacob's wife, not Rachel, and there would be nothing that Rachel could do about it.

It doesn't work out like that, of course. Jacob doesn't meekly accept the swap that's been forced upon him. He's not satisfied with one sister instead of the other. He's a man of honour, so he won't send Leah away. But he still wants Rachel. He still loves Rachel.

Leah gets a head start in her marriage. But seven days is little enough time to make her husband fall in love with her after he's spent seven years patiently working to earn the sister he fell in love with. For seven further years, she has to watch Jacob work even more patiently. Seven years while he bears politely with her and looks eagerly at Rachel. Seven years of that knife being twisted a little deeper each day.

It's hard not to compare yourself with other people. It's hard to grow up with your prettier, younger, more beloved sister and not compare yourself with her. It's hard to live as an adult with your husband's prettier, younger, more beloved wife and not compare yourself with her. It's hard to be Leah.

And yet.

And yet it's Leah who continues to be blessed. Leah who gives birth to a daughter and two more sons while Rachel still has none. A further two sons follow from Leah's servant (also by Jacob), and Leah gives the younger of those the name Asher, saying 'Happy am I! The women will call me happy' (Genesis 30:13). But it's also Leah who calls her own sixth son Zebulun. She says, 'God has presented me with a precious gift. This time my husband will treat me with honour, because I have borne him six sons' (Genesis 30:20).

Jacob does honour Leah. And God blesses Leah, both with children and with contentment. So much so that now it's Rachel who compares herself with her elder, plainer sister and finds herself lacking.

Leah

For reflection

- With whom do you compare yourself? In what ways does that person seem to have been more blessed than you?
- Examine your own life to see how God has blessed you and give thanks for that.

Prayer

Lord God,
thank you for all the wonderful ways you have blessed my life,
for all the reasons I have to be happy,
for all the evidence of your love for me,
and for all the joy and pleasure that I know.
Help me always to be satisfied in you
and to be content in every circumstance.
Amen.

19

7

Dinah

When Shechem son of Hamor the Hivite, the ruler of that area,
saw her, he took her and raped her.
(Genesis 34:2)

Bible reading: Genesis 34:1–31

Plenty of the women in this list have their own #MeToo story. There
was Hagar, remember, given to Abram by her mistress. Leah and
Rachel both do the same with the enslaved women, Bilhah and
Zilpah, sending them in to have sex with Jacob. Twice, Sarah herself
was told to pretend she was Abraham's sister, and was left to the
mercy of foreign rulers.

Because our Bibles don't often use the word 'rape', we can easily
let ourselves skim over stories like these. But none of these women
was given a choice. All of them were used by people more powerful
than they were. They stood to lose their homes, their workplaces,
their communities and their good names: they were compelled to
obey. Maybe there was physical force and violence, and maybe there
was not. It doesn't matter. Those women's bodies were used by men
in ways that they had not chosen.

But because we don't have the word 'rape' in those passages, it is
all the more shocking when we get to Genesis 34:2 and we are told
that when Shechem saw Dinah, 'he took her and raped her'. This
must be even worse than what happened to Hagar, to Sarah, and to
Bilhah and Zilpah. This wasn't a question of consent unspoken. This
was something more violent, more horrific, more violating.

Shechem rapes her once, then decides he wants more of the same.
We're told that his heart was drawn to Dinah; that he loved the young

woman and spoke tenderly to her. He decides he wants her for his wife.

But notice what we aren't told. We aren't told that her heart was drawn to him. We're not told that she loved him or spoke tenderly to him. We're not told that she wants him for her husband.

Dinah is lucky. She has men who do care about her and protect her. She is part of a family, a household. She has brothers. They pretend to accept Shechem's proposal; they lure Shechem's people in, stipulating only – only, hah! – that they must get circumcised. And then they avenge their sister.

So, Simeon and Levi kill Shechem, his father and all the men of their city. They plunder and loot the city, and they bring the women and children back with them.

When Rachael Denhollander, a US lawyer, former gymnast and survivor of sexual abuse, spoke at the sentencing of Larry Nassar, the doctor who abused dozens and dozens of young American gymnasts, she asked the question, 'How much is a little girl worth?' She answered her own question this way, 'These victims are worth everything . . . I plead with you to impose the maximum sentence under the plea agreement because everything is what these survivors are worth.'[1]

Simeon and Levi knew what their sister was worth. Jacob was worried about what they had done, worried about repercussions and worried they had gone too far; Simeon and Levi were not: 'But they replied, "Should he have treated our sister like a prostitute?"' (Genesis 34:31).

How much was Dinah worth? How much is a girl worth? How much is a woman worth?

Everything.

1 'Rachael Denhollander: "So, I ask, how much is a little girl worth?", victim impact statement, Larry Nassar sentencing – 2018', Speakola (2018), <https://speakola.com/ideas/rachael-denhollander-larry-nassar-sentencing-2018>, accessed 2 August 2021.

For reflection

- Have you ever witnessed a woman being sexually harassed or abused? How did you respond?
- Have you ever been treated in a way that made you feel worthless? What difference would it have made if someone else had stood up for you?

Prayer

Dear Father,
we praise you that in your sight no one is worthless:
no child,
no girl,
no woman,
no victim of abuse.
Help us to be courageous in standing up against abusers,
against bullies,
against rapists,
and in standing up for those who are vulnerable,
naive,
weak
or young,
as you have called us to do in your name.
Amen.

8

Tamar

'She is more righteous than I, since I wouldn't give her to my
son Shelah.'
(Genesis 38:26)

Bible reading: Genesis 38:1–30

Rape. Infertility. Rivalry. More rape. And we're still in Genesis. It's
not exactly family-friendly reading, is it?

And yet, of course, family is the whole point. These women we've
been reading about are all fighting for the family. Fighting to keep
the family going through the generations. Fighting for their own
place and their sons' inheritance within it. Fighting for the protection and honour of the people in it.

And so today we have another story that isn't exactly family-
friendly. Another woman fighting for her right to be counted as part
of the family. Another family full of tragedy and trauma.

It starts so straightforwardly. Judah marries and his wife has three
sons: Er, Onan and Shelah. Three fine sons. Heirs to carry his name
through the generations. Three fine, wicked, selfish sons. Judah finds
a suitable wife to marry his eldest son, Er, but before Tamar can fall
pregnant by him, God puts wicked Er to death.

No problem. There are two more sons to go. Tamar is married
again, this time to the second son, Onan. Selfish Onan who doesn't
want his first son to be counted as belonging to his elder brother.
Selfish Onan who will go and lie with his wife, but make sure never
to get her pregnant. Selfish, wicked Onan who goes the same way as
Er: he is put to death by the Lord.

No problem. There's still one more son after all.

But Judah doesn't want his third son to go the way of the first two. He decides it's Tamar who has to go. She must be the one who is dangerous, poisonous, and has brought only harm to his two fine sons. He knows that he ought to marry her to Shelah, his third son. He ought to keep her in his household, his family. But he won't. Judah sends Tamar away. He sends her back to her own father.

He cuts her out of the family.

Oh, sure, he promises he'll send for her to return. He promises she'll marry Shelah one day. But that day never comes: 'For she saw that, though Shelah had now grown up, she had not been given to him as his wife' (Genesis 38:14).

Tamar knows her rights. Tamar knows her place. Tamar is going to fight for her place in the family, whatever it takes.

Tamar is bold and she is brave. She isn't afraid to act shamelessly in order to shame her father-in-law. She may be the one disguising herself as a shrine-prostitute, but he's the one actually paying for sex with a shrine-prostitute. She may be the one pregnant and unmarried, but he's the one who has broken his promises to his family.

And amazingly, in the end, Tamar isn't shamed for her actions. She isn't blamed for his actions.

Even Judah himself admits, 'She is more righteous than I, since I wouldn't give her to my son Shelah' (Genesis 38:26).

Righteous indeed. She is Tamar, the mother of Perez and Zerah. Tamar, whose descendant, David, some nine generations later, will be the first to sit on the throne in Jerusalem. Tamar who will be the first of just three women to be named in the genealogy of Christ (Matthew 1:3).

Tamar who would not let any man take away her right to be counted in the family of God's people.

For reflection

- How far would you go to make sure that you were counted among the family of God's people?
- What has it cost you already? Has it been worth it?

Prayer

Lord God,
thank you for Tamar's faith,
which would not let her give up her place among your people,
no matter what it cost her.
May our faith be as bold and brave as Tamar's;
may we hold on to our right to be called children of God,
no matter what it costs us,
for we know the heavenly reward that is to come
through Tamar's son,
Jesus Christ our Lord.
Amen.

9

Shiphrah and Puah

The midwives, however, feared God and did not do what the king of Egypt had told them to do; they let the boys live. (Exodus 1:17)

Bible reading: Exodus 1:15–21

I'm a rule-keeper by nature. I just think rules are basically a good thing for any society. Rules set a level playing field: they tell us how to get where we want; they keep us all safe. But not all rules are a good thing. Even natural rule-keepers know that sometimes the right thing to do is break the rule.

Such as when the king of Egypt comes up with a new rule for the Israelite midwives, Shiphrah and Puah. He tells them that, when they assist the Hebrew mothers to give birth, they must kill all the male babies that are born. The girls don't matter, obviously. The girls are no threat. The girls can live.

Shiphrah and Puah aren't in the business of killing babies. They are midwives. Their job is to save babies and to help women as they give birth.

Their refusal to obey is more than that, though. These women may be Israelites, enslaved in Egypt, but they know that the king of Egypt is not their ultimate authority: 'The midwives, however, feared God and did not do what the king of Egypt had told them to do; they let the boys live' (Exodus 1:17).

They won't kill the boys. They won't do it because it's wrong. And they won't do it because they care more about what God thinks than what the king of Egypt says.

These brave women won't do what Pharaoh says and they'll even lie to him about it. They tell the king that it's impossible, rather than just telling him they refuse. Their lie is not only to protect themselves, I think, but also to stop Pharaoh from sending another pair of midwives to do the same gruesome job.

The Egyptian king – presumably ignorant of the reality of childbirth – believes their lie and doesn't have them punished. More than that, 'God was kind to the midwives and the people increased and became even more numerous. And because the midwives feared God, he gave them families of their own' (Exodus 1:21–22). God rewards the Israelites because of the faith of these women, whom he rewards too, blessing them with children.

I don't know how many baby boys' lives were saved by Shiphrah and Puah, but even if it had been only one, their actions would have been heroic. They risked themselves, their freedom, even perhaps their own lives. Shiphrah and Puah – foreign women, enslaved women – stood up to the king, disobeyed him and deceived him. And because of them, those babies lived.

Rules are good, except when they aren't.

Obey the law, except when it's wicked.

Honour the authorities, but not more than you honour God himself.

For reflection

- Are you a natural rule-keeper or a natural rule-breaker? How can you determine when it may be good and right to break the rules?
- Many Christians today live under oppressive anti-Christian regimes. In what situations might it be right and good for them to deceive and disobey the authorities? Pray that they may be wise in their actions.

Prayer

Almighty God,
thank you that we do not live under the oppression of slavery
and that we do not face the terror of genocide.
We pray for our Christian brothers and sisters
who are living in fear for their lives,
who are subject to laws that force them to deny their faith
in words or in actions.
Give them the courage of Shiphrah and Puah
to do what is right in your eyes
and, in your kindness, reward them with great blessings
to the glory of Christ.
Amen.

10

Pharaoh's daughter

She opened it and saw the baby. He was crying, and she felt sorry for him. 'This is one of the Hebrew babies,' she said. (Exodus 2:6)

Bible reading: Exodus 2:1–10

Confession time: I don't really like babies. I know, I know. I'm sure yours is beautiful and adorable and perfect, but they just aren't my thing. They're mostly not all that pretty, in my opinion. Especially not when they're screaming. Or pooing. And if they're not doing those, they're generally sleeping. So, yeah. Don't put me in charge of the crèche.

But even I find that babies bring out a protective instinct in me. They're so helpless. So vulnerable. And when they open their eyes wide and just look at you, I admit, it's hard to resist.

Pharaoh's daughter couldn't resist. She's gone down to the river with her entourage of maidservants in attendance. And there it is: a basket, left among the reeds. She's curious. I don't suppose there were many picnickers on the banks of the Nile in those days. Who would have left a basket there?

So the maid is sent to get the basket. They open it up and there's the baby. Crying.

Pharaoh's daughter immediately knows where he's come from. She lives in the palace. She hears what her father is doing. This must be one of the Hebrew babies. One of the babies that was supposed to have been killed. One of the babies that her own father had ordered to be killed.

But . . . it's a baby. He's helpless. He's vulnerable. He's needy.

And when she looks down at him, her protective instinct kicks in. Pharaoh's daughter can't save all the Hebrew boys, but she can save this one. She can take him into the safest place in the country – into the Pharaoh's own palace, and she'll raise him as if he were her own son. Her father won't say no to her.

As she looks at him, she realizes he's such a small baby that he'll need a wet nurse. Conveniently, the young Hebrew girl who just happens to be standing nearby offers to find one for her so that, in the end, it's Moses' mother who gets to look after him anyway. You couldn't make it up.

This baby has an extraordinary group of women helping him to survive against all the odds:

Shiphrah and Puah, who refused to kill the babies they had
    helped to be born.
The Levite woman who refused to destroy her own baby.
His sister, sent to watch over him.
The maidservant who took the basket out of the river.
Pharaoh's daughter, who was moved to take him to safety
    and raise him as her own.

This baby, of course, is Moses: Moses who will go on to lead God's people out of slavery and out of Egypt, Moses who will be the mediator between God and his people, Moses who will establish God's law among the people.

The rest of the book of Exodus will tell us all about Moses and God's extraordinary saving acts accomplished through him. But these first two chapters of Exodus are all about the women. All of them bravely doing the right thing. Desperately doing the right thing. Compassionately doing the right thing.

And after all, it's such an ordinary thing. Every day, women all over the world are helping others to give birth. Every day, women all over the world are keeping their babies safe. Every day, women all over the world are watching over their younger brothers and sisters. And, every day, women all over the world are caring for other people's children as if they were their own.

Every day, women all over the world are doing something amazing.

For reflection

- Who are the women who have done amazing things in your life? Give thanks to God for them.
- Who are the children you know of who need protection, care and compassion? How can you do something amazing for them?

Prayer

Heavenly Father,
thank you for all the women who are heroes,
all the women who are doing amazing things,
all the women caring for their children,
protecting them from harm,
and all the women raising other people's children as their own,
providing for all their needs.
Thank you for the women who have made sacrifices,
taken risks
and shown compassion.
Thank you that you see the work of these women.
Teach us to honour this work as you do.
Amen.

11

Zipporah

But Zipporah took a flint knife, cut off her son's foreskin and touched Moses' feet with it. 'Surely you are a bridegroom of blood to me,' she said. So the LORD let him alone.
(Exodus 4:25–26)

Bible reading: Exodus 4:18–26

Marrying a foreigner is a risky business in the Old Testament. Sometimes it works out well, as it did for Boaz when he married Ruth. And sometimes it's a disaster, as it was for Solomon when he married the daughter of the Pharaoh of his day, followed by countless other foreign women. But for Moses, his marriage to the woman from Midian, Zipporah, seems to have saved his life.

He's come home from meeting Yahweh in the bush that burned but wasn't destroyed and now he's got to return to Egypt, to the land where he was born and raised. He's got to go back to the place from which he fled in fear when it became known that he had killed an Egyptian man for beating up one of Moses' fellow Israelites.

God is now sending Moses back to rescue those fellow Israelites from their Egyptian enslavers.

Moses isn't going back on his own. During his time in Midian, he has acquired a wife and a family. So now, he is taking his family with him. Zipporah and her sons are loaded on to a donkey and head for a land that is wholly foreign to them. Their only link to Egypt or Israel is the man who walks beside them, Moses, carrying the staff that God has given him.

But the journey takes a while and they have to stop overnight. It's here, as they break the journey, that Zipporah faces the terrifying moment of seeing her husband about to die. About to be killed by the very God who told him to go to Egypt.

It's not the first time Moses' life has been at risk, of course. And it's not the first time that a woman has saved him.

This time it is Zipporah who steps in to save her husband's life. She does the obvious thing:

But Zipporah took a flint knife, cut off her son's foreskin and touched Moses' feet with it. 'Surely you are a bridegroom of blood to me,' she said. So, the LORD let him alone. (At that time she said 'bridegroom of blood', referring to circumcision.) (Exodus 4:25–26)

I mean, your guess is as good as mine.

Circumcision, of course, was a sign of the covenant God had made hundreds of years previously with Abraham and his descendants. As a result of that, presumably Moses had been circumcised as a baby while he was still living with his Hebrew family. But, from this story, it seems that Moses' sons had not.

Perhaps God's action against Moses was because his family did not bear that covenant sign, because they still lived as Midianites rather than Israelites. Because his sons were not marked as members of God's chosen people nor acknowledged to be descendants of Abraham and heirs of the covenant promises.

Perhaps Zipporah's action signifies her commitment to Moses' God, to Moses' people. Perhaps her husband has, after all, told her about his God during the years they have been married. Perhaps her husband has explained why he himself is circumcised. Perhaps he's told her what that means and of the promises he bears in the scars on his body. Perhaps Zipporah has been listening and learning. Perhaps she has begun believing.

Whatever is going on, it works. The circumcision of her son, the foreskin touched to the feet of Moses, the bridegroom of blood: it works. The blood propitiates God's anger against Moses. The blood from the circumcision keeps him safe. Gives him life.

Moses is Zipporah's bridegroom, her husband. Now he becomes a 'bridegroom of blood'.

We too have a bridegroom, of course. A bridegroom of blood. Blood from his circumcision. Blood that poured from his side. Blood that propitiates God's anger against us. Keeps us safe. Gives us life.

I have no idea how Zipporah knew what to do. But I know she did the right thing.

For reflection

- Has God ever called you to a particular path and then set obstacles in your way? Why do you think he might do this?
- Old covenant religion was often a bloody business that involved circumcision, sacrifices and death. Why is blood so significant and how do we continue to recognize that in new covenant faith?

Prayer

God of Abraham, Isaac and Jacob,
God of the Israelites and God of the whole world,
we deserve nothing from you but your wrath,
and yet you are a God who graciously has mercy on us,
who faithfully keeps his covenant promises,
and who sent his own Son to be a bridegroom of blood for us
to save us and to give us life.
May we never lose sight of all that it cost you
to make us your people.
May we always be willing to give whatever you demand of us
as our living sacrifice of praise.
Amen.

12

Miriam

Then Miriam the prophet, Aaron's sister, took a tambourine in her hand, and all the women followed her, with tambourines and dancing.
(Exodus 15:20)

Bible reading: Numbers 12:1–16

He's always been the special one. Even when you were a little girl, you were told that you had to look after him. You were sent to watch over him when your mum put him in the river. You were the one who stepped forward to make sure that your mother was allowed to keep caring for him even after Pharaoh's daughter had decided to adopt him. Moses is your little brother, and he's always been special. Different. Set apart. You've always known that.

And now he's back. Back from his self-imposed exile, with a wife and a family of his own. Now he's back and apparently God sent him to lead the Israelites out of Egypt. You're not surprised that it took a while for the Israelites to believe him. He's always lived a gilded life; he's always been set apart from the rest of the Hebrews. He's never been beaten by a slave master to make him work harder for less reward. What does he know?

But he has come back and it seems that God is with him after all. He has come with God's staff in his hand and God's word in his mouth. Him and Aaron, your other brother.

And you.

Because you're a prophet too.

Because God speaks through you, just as he does through your brothers. And on that day – when Moses had led all the people through the Red Sea on dry ground, between towering walls of water, and then he led everyone in singing praise to God – your voice was finally heard too. You were singing too. You were leading all the women in their praise to God.

You see? Moses isn't that special after all. He's married to a foreigner for a start. And yes, fine, God speaks through him but, as you and Aaron point out to each other, God has spoken through the two of you as well. You decide to confront Moses about it. But instead God calls all three of you, the two brothers and the sister, and he is going to confront you about it.

You, Miriam, stand before God, with your two brothers, and hear his voice. And suddenly, you realize, it is different. Moses *is* different. Special. Set apart. For while you have heard God speak, as he does to all his prophets, you have not stood face to face with the living God. You have not gone up the mountain into the cloud. You have not even taken off your sandals to come near the holy ground of the burning bush.

You have stood at the bottom of the mountain with everyone else, trembling and terrified. Because God's holiness *is* terrifying.

And so now, as you stand there, and the Lord's anger burns against you – you, personally; you, Miriam – you realize that you have sinned. And not just against your brother, Moses. You have sinned against your God, Yahweh. You have sinned by calling into question how he has chosen to speak to his people. You have sinned against God by thinking yourself more important than you are. You have been foolish and you have been sinful and you need to learn humility.

God sends his judgment on you, turning your skin white and flaky with the unmistakeable signs of leprosy. Uncleanness. Exclusion.

There is the humility. You can't do anything. Aaron can't do anything. But he turns to Moses and asks for help. And Moses, holding no grudge, turns to the Lord, on behalf of you, his sister, and prays, 'Please, God, heal her!' (Numbers 12:13).

We also have a brother who holds no grudges, and who is a better mediator between God and his people even than Moses. We have a brother we can't claim to be equal with but whose humility exceeds our own. We have a brother we can turn to, no matter how foolish or sinful we have been. We have a brother who intercedes for us, crying to the Lord, 'Please, God, heal her!'

For reflection

- Whom are you envious of? Whose position or status do you covet? What place do you think should have been yours?
- What do you need to repent of and where do you need to learn humility?

Prayer

Lord Jesus,
you have called us your brothers and sisters,
and so we dare to ask you to plead on our behalf to the Father,
asking him to heal us,
to forgive us,
to restore us,
to transform us.
Thank you that you hold no grudges against us,
and that you live ever to intercede for us
in the Most Holy Place.
We turn to you.
Amen.

13

Mahlah. Noah. Hoglah. Milkah. Tirzah.

What Zelophehad's daughters are saying is right. You must certainly give them property as an inheritance among their father's relatives and give their father's inheritance to them. (Numbers 27:7)

Bible reading: Numbers 27:1–11

I love watching *Who Do You Think You Are?* on TV. At first, I couldn't see the point of it: why would I be interested in the family history of minor celebrities? But then I watched a couple of episodes and I suddenly realized why people found it so fascinating. It's not because it's about minor celebrities; it's because it's about *people*. It's about people knowing where they have come from, and understanding more of their history and often about how that history has an impact on the present. It's about knowing whom they belong to and whom they are connected to. Sometimes the genealogists discover a living relative whom no one had known about, whom the celebrity can meet. More often, it's just the stories from the past that make the ancestors come alive.

It's interesting to me that so few of us these days do know where we come from. Beyond grandparents or perhaps great-grandparents, most of us are very fuzzy about our family history. But for the Israelites, it was essential knowledge. You had to know that you belonged. That you were a descendant of Abraham and an heir of the promise. Their genealogies could be recited back through many, many generations.

And so it was for Mahlah, Noah, Hoglah, Milkah and Tirzah. They knew where they had come from: their father was Zelophehad; their grandfather was Hepher; their great-grandfather was Gilead; their great-great-grandfather was Makir; and their great-great-great-grandfather was Manasseh. And so their great-great-great-great-grandfather was Joseph, son of Jacob, son of Isaac, son of Abraham.

They did not need a *Who Do You Think You Are?* researcher to tell them that they belonged. They were part of the family, the clan, the tribe and the nation.

But they didn't have a brother. And without a brother, Zelophehad's name would be forgotten. No one would list him in their family because that line would always be remembered through the male line of ancestors, not through his daughters. Even if all five girls had children, not one of them would be remembered as Zelophehad's descendants.

These sisters knew that their father was a good man. He may have died in the wilderness, but not because he was rebellious. Not because he set himself up against the Lord. He deserved to keep his place in the family. In the history.

So they went to Moses themselves, because they had no one else to speak for them, and they made their case: 'Why should our father's name disappear from his clan because he had no son? Give us property among our father's relatives' (Numbers 27:4).

Moses takes the case to God and God, it turns out, takes the women's side: 'What Zelophehad's daughters are saying is right. You must certainly give them property as an inheritance among their father's relatives and give their father's inheritance to them' (Numbers 27:7).

The property and the inheritance will pass to Zelophehad's daughters and his name will not be forgotten. The women are their father's children and it is their right.

There's even a new law given to establish this right for all women in Israel. Because the women belong too. They belong to the family, the clan, the tribe and the nation. Because Israel's history is their history. Because their father's name should not be forgotten.

And neither should theirs.

Mahlah.

Noah.

Hoglah.

Milkah.

Tirzah.

For reflection

- Where do you come from? What is your story? What is your history?
- In what way are all Christians 'descendants of Abraham and heirs of the promise'? Why is this important?

Prayer

Heavenly Father,

thank you that, in Christ, we too have been grafted

into this family tree of God's covenant people,

that we have been counted as heirs of the promise

that this history is our history,

and that this story is our story.

Teach us not to forget those who came before us,

those who passed down the promises

and those who taught us the gospel.

As we honour them, we give all the praise to you,

our Father and our God.

Amen.

14

Rahab

'When we heard of it, our hearts melted in fear and everyone's courage failed because of you, for the LORD your God is God in heaven above and on the earth below.'
(Joshua 2:11, NIV2011)

Bible reading: Joshua 2:1–13

The fear of the Lord is the beginning of wisdom (Proverbs 9:10).

Fear of the Lord recognizes that God is God, that he is all-powerful, that he is Almighty.

Fear of the Lord causes hearts to melt and knees to tremble, and mouths to dry and men to bow down.

Rahab feared the Lord.

Rahab, safe within the walls of the city of Jericho, had heard the stories of this shambolic group in the wilderness whose God had somehow enabled them to defeat the organized armies of Sihon and Og. No doubt the stories about these runaway slaves had been told and told again: stories about how their God had enabled them to break out of the iron grip of Egypt's Pharaoh and make a bid for freedom by walking through the Red Sea on dry ground. Perhaps there were even rumours swirling that these Hebrews were planning – even though they were taking their time about it – to come to conquer Canaan. Maybe the citizens of Jericho had even speculated that the invasion would begin right there, with their city.

Rahab had certainly heard the stories. Rahab had felt the fear. And Rahab knew that the Israelites' God was God indeed: 'When we heard of it, our hearts melted in fear and every-one's courage failed because of you, for the LORD your God is God in heaven above and on the earth below' (Joshua 2:11, NIV2011).

The Lord, *your* God, is God in heaven above and on the earth below.

Their God, the God of the Israelites, is God in heaven above and on the earth below.

He may be the God of this ramshackle tribe in the desert, but Rahab has worked out something far more important: he is also the God of heaven and earth. He is the God of all people everywhere. In other words: their God *is* God.

What do you do when you are confronted with this God and realize that you are on the wrong side of him? What do you do when your courage fails and you are afraid?

You change your allegiance, of course. You throw your lot in with his. You disobey your own king; you hide the Israelite spies; and you plead with them for mercy on you and your family. You decide you don't want to be a Canaanite any more. You want to be on God's side.

Rahab does just that. She pleads for her life to be spared and the lives of those she loves. She demands a sign that will protect her on the day when her city will be destroyed. Instead of losing her life, she will save it.

The fear of the Lord is the beginning of wisdom for Rahab. It prompts her to switch her allegiance, to defy her king, and to seek mercy and protection for herself and her family.

And that really was only the beginning. She lived out the rest of her years on earth as a faithful Israelite and her memory lived on much longer. Rahab is honoured as one of the handful of women mentioned by name in the ancestry of Christ himself. In the New Testament, she is honoured for her faith in the book of Hebrews and for her righteousness in the letter of James.

Here's the thing about Rahab: it doesn't matter, in the end, whether you first turn to God out of love or whether you turn to him out of fear. What matters is that the God you turn to is the Lord, who is God in heaven above and on the earth below. Throw yourself on his mercy and he will not let you fall.

For reflection

- Think about how you first came to God. Was it prompted by fear or by love – or both? Does that make any difference to your trust in him now?
- What have we to fear from the Lord today? Who should be fearful of him?

Prayer

Lord God of heaven and earth,
thank you for Rahab, who did not fear the soldiers or her king,
who did not fear to lose her people and her place in life,
but who rightly feared you, the all-powerful God,
and whose fear caused her to throw herself on your mercy.
May we follow her example, not fearing the world,
nor anything we may lose or suffer,
but having only that fear of the Lord which brings us to true
    wisdom.
Amen.

15

Deborah

'Certainly I will go with you,' said Deborah. 'But because of
the course you are taking, the honour will not be yours, for the
LORD will deliver Sisera into the hands of a woman.'
(Judges 4:9)

Bible reading: Judges 4:1–15

It's not supposed to be Deborah.

Deborah, like Miriam before her, is a prophet. She can make good
judgments in disputes between Israelites. She's perfectly happy
sitting under her tree, holding court.

It's tough, of course, because the Israelites are going through one
of their regular phases of great wickedness now that they are settled
in the land of Canaan. There are plenty of disputes to be sorted out.
There is plenty of God's wisdom needed and doubtless plenty of it
ignored.

It's tough because of Sisera too. The Canaanite king, Jabin, is cruel
and harsh and has a huge army, led by the mighty Sisera, which keeps
the Israelites firmly under his thumb. And so finally, *finally*, the
Israelites realize that they need to ask for help. Not from Deborah,
obviously. No, they need the Lord's help.

But look, she knows the pattern. This isn't their first time through
this cycle of wickedness, oppression and finally crying out for help.
Help always comes in the form of a judge. Not a judge sitting in a law
court but a judge leading his people to victory over their enemies. So
Deborah looks around for the answer to Israel's prayers and she finds
Barak. He should be the one to lead Israel's army up against Sisera's
so that God will give them victory and rest from their enemies.

Barak, it turns out, is something of a coward: 'If you go with me, I will go; but if you don't go with me, I won't go' (Judges 4:8).

Maybe he hopes that she won't go. She's a woman after all.

Deborah, it turns out, is no coward: '"Certainly I will go with you," said Deborah. "But because of the course you are taking, the honour will not be yours, for the LORD will deliver Sisera into the hands of a woman"' (Judges 4:9).

In the Old Testament, it's always a sign that something is very wrong when men won't do their job and women have to step up and take their place. It's not that the women aren't capable. It's not that the women are usurpers. The problem is with the men. The problem is that, in these situations, they are fearful, cowardly, lazy and rebellious. They don't trust God or they won't trust God.

That doesn't stop God from keeping his promises and fulfilling his plans. But the consequence for Barak is that he will not take any of the glory for the victory. He will not be the one to defeat Sisera.

Deborah will go with Barak to raise an army and lead it against Sisera's troops. Deborah's trust will be proved worthy, when God gives them the victory. Deborah's prophecy will be proved true, when the Lord delivers Sisera into the hands of a woman.

Maybe it should have been Barak. But, as it turns out, Deborah was certainly up to the job.

For reflection

- Why are we so slow to recognize when we need the Lord's help and so slow to cry out to him?
- How have you responded to the Lord's call in your life? With faith and courage or with fear and rebellion?

Prayer

Lord God,
grant us faith that turns to you first;
faith that responds with courage and obedience;

faith that looks to you for victory;
and faith that finds its rest in you.
Amen.

16

Jael

But Jael, Heber's wife, picked up a tent peg and a hammer
and went quietly to him while he lay fast asleep, exhausted.
She drove the peg through his temple into the ground, and he
died.
(Judges 4:21)

Bible reading: Judges 4:16–24

Yesterday, I mentioned Deborah's prophecy that Sisera would be
delivered into the hands of a woman. Indeed he was. But that woman
was not Deborah. It was Jael.

When the Israelite troops attacked Sisera's army of chariots, it
soon became clear that it was going to be a rout. The Israelites were
destroying their enemies. Sisera, their leader, did not stay to be
destroyed. He got down from his chariot and fled on foot.

He fled to a safe place, to the tent of one of his allies, where he
could hide and lick his wounds. He fled to a place where there was
no one to fear.

There was just a woman there. Just Jael, inviting him in, telling
him not to be afraid, giving him a blanket to rest under. Just Jael,
generously giving him milk when he'd asked only for some water.

And so Sisera lay down and slept, weary and exhausted after the
battle and his escape. He slept because he was safe. Because he
trusted that Jael would guard the tent. He trusted that, if necessary,
Jael would lie for him and pretend there was no one inside.

But Jael was no ally of Sisera's, even though her husband was.
Perhaps Jael knew of Sisera's cruelty in oppressing the Israelites. Perhaps, like Rahab generations earlier, she'd heard about the

Israelite God and knew him to be the Lord of the heavens above and the earth below.

So, while Sisera was sleeping, when he was most vulnerable, she picked up her weapons: the tent peg and the hammer. And she did not lack either the courage or the strength to use them.

When Barak, the leader of the Israelite army came past, she went out to meet him. '"Come," she said, "I will show you the man you're looking for." So he went in with her, and there lay Sisera with the tent peg through his temple – dead' (Judges 4:22).

There is a lesson here, isn't there, for those who are powerful, strong and enemies of God. There is a lesson about making assumptions concerning the loyalties of those who are weaker and inconsequential. There is a lesson here for many men and, I daresay, quite a number of women. The lesson is this: don't assume that the woman minding her own business at home is no threat. Don't assume she'll do what she's told. Don't assume that her husband speaks for her. Don't assume that she isn't brave or that she isn't strong. Remember that 'God chose the weak things of the world to shame the strong' (1 Corinthians 1:27), and take care not to be put to shame.

Perhaps there is a lesson here too for those who are weak, vulnerable and overlooked. Perhaps there is a lesson for those of us who feel inadequate and afraid, knowing that nothing we do could be of consequence to the almighty God. The lesson is this: don't assume that the mighty leader of the great army (with all its chariots and horses), the man with all the wealth and power, the tyrant and the oppressor – don't assume that he will be victorious in the end. Don't assume that he is invulnerable. Don't assume that you are too weak, too insignificant and too female to defeat him. Remember that 'God chose the weak things of the world to shame the strong' (1 Corinthians 1:27), and take care not to be put to shame.

Because you never know when that powerful tyrant will turn out to be Sisera and that inconsequential housewife will prove herself to be Jael.

For reflection

- What situations do you feel powerless to change and which people do you feel too intimidated to confront?
- How might God use the weak things of the world to shame the strong in those situations?

Prayer

Almighty God,
King of kings and Lord of lords,
ruler of heaven and earth,
may your power be demonstrated
through our weakness.
May we fear no one,
knowing that you are with us.
May we always do what is right,
without fear or shame.
For your glory.
Amen.

17

Delilah

'See if you can lure him into showing you the secret of his great strength and how we can overpower him so we may tie him up and subdue him. Each one of us will give you eleven hundred shekels of silver.'
(Judges 16:5)

Bible reading: Judges 16:4–22

Love makes us all vulnerable. Maybe that's even what love is: willingly making yourself vulnerable to someone else. Letting them in deeply enough to change you, to touch you and to hurt you.

Love made Samson vulnerable. The great and mighty hero, Samson was the strong man who had been known to tear apart the city gate with his bare hands. He'd been blessed by God since his birth. He was clever and handsome, and everything he wanted fell into his lap. He seemed invulnerable.

But he'd been stung before. His first wife, a Philistine woman, had tried to coax his secrets out of him so that the Philistines could use them against him. The plan backfired and she ended up being used by them in revenge against him. He'd liked his first wife well enough – she'd been his own choice – but she'd turned out to be a bad choice for him.

So there's Samson: strong and mighty on the outside, but a little bit sore and tender on the inside. And there's Delilah: a Philistine woman from the valley of Sorek, but a beautiful woman nonetheless.

Samson falls in love.

Delilah, on the other hand, sees an opportunity.

The Philistines want to know Samson's weak point. He's too strong for them and too clever for them, and he's repeatedly proved that. But surely he'll tell Delilah how he can be defeated. He loves her. He'll make himself vulnerable to her.

For eleven hundred shekels of silver from every Philistine ruler, Delilah will do it.

She's not subtle about it in her first approach to him: 'Tell me the secret of your great strength and how you can be tied up and subdued' (Judges 16:6).

Samson is not going to let another woman be his undoing after what happened in his first marriage. So he lies to her. And again the next night. And the next.

But Delilah is not giving up. Just think of all those lovely silver shekels that will be hers. One way or another, she'll get him to tell her his secret. Nagging and prodding and poking him about it every day 'until he was sick to death of it' (Judges 16:16). Like a dripping tap, she wears away at him until, in the end, he gives in.

This is Delilah's moment. She sends for the Philistines and a barber. And the moment Samson is asleep, she acts. She exposes his weakness through her persistent nagging. She waits for him to sleep to expose it further. And she exploits his weakness, calling on the Philistine leaders to take advantage of him.

If only he hadn't loved Delilah. If only he hadn't laid himself bare, exposing his deepest weaknesses and trusting her not to exploit them.

And for what?

I daresay those silver shekels made a hard pillow for Delilah to rest her head on each night.

For reflection

- How does love make you vulnerable? Does your love for Christ make you vulnerable?
- Why is money such a powerful temptation for people? Where do you need to guard against that temptation in your life?

Prayer

Lord Jesus,
thank you for your love,
which was so strong you were willing to make yourself vulnerable,
even vulnerable to death.
Thank you that loving you
never means making ourselves vulnerable,
because we know that you will never take advantage;
you will never betray us;
and you will never harm us.
May we rest secure in that love for ever.
Amen.

18

The concubine

So the man took his concubine and sent her outside to them, and they raped her and abused her throughout the night, and at dawn they let her go. At daybreak the woman went back to the house where her master was staying, fell down at the door and lay there until daylight.

(Judges 19:25–26)

Bible reading: Judges 19:1–30

There are some things about this woman that are very difficult to pin down. She's described as a concubine but, for the most part, she's treated as a wife and, in the absence of any other wife, it's hard to understand why she had the secondary status of a concubine.

She's said to have been unfaithful to her husband, but it's not absolutely clear that this took the form of sexual adultery. What we do know is that she left him and went home to her parents. Maybe that was the 'unfaithfulness'. She had left her father's household for marriage, so perhaps simply returning to it could have been interpreted as unfaithfulness to her husband.

Certainly, the Levite husband cared enough about this woman to go to her father's house to persuade her to return. Not immediately, admittedly, which suggests that whatever the source of their quarrel, it was serious. Maybe it was adultery after all. But he is not finished with her, whatever she has done.

Her family welcome him. They still consider him to be her husband. They like him and they keep persuading him to stay longer. Perhaps they are sorry to say farewell to their daughter again. But in the end, he must go home and he must take his wife with him.

It's on that journey that their world ends.

It's in Gibeah, a town belonging to the Israelite tribe of Benjamin, where no one will give their fellow Israelites shelter for the night. No one will offer basic hospitality. The couple aren't asking for much – they have food and provisions with them – but they need a bed and a roof. Every door should have been opened to them. Not in Gibeah.

Eventually, one older man offers them shelter. But he is unable to protect them from the wickedness of the city. Just as, centuries earlier, a mob had banged on Lot's door in Sodom, demanding that he send out his visitors to be raped, so now a mob bangs on the door of this old man, demanding that he send out his male visitor to be raped.

And just as Lot went out to appease the crowd by offering his own daughters, so this old man goes out to appease the crowd by offering his daughter and his guest's concubine. Lot was lucky. His guests dragged him back inside; they protected his household and enabled them all to escape the city before it was destroyed.

This time, there is no such protection. The concubine is sent out to be used and abused and raped and left for dead.

Gibeah, you see, has become Sodom. But there is no caveat for those in Gibeah as there had been for those in Sodom; the Lord didn't promise to save any righteous people who might be found (see Genesis 18:16–32).

Maybe there were no righteous people here to save. Perhaps the concubine was indeed an adulterous woman. Maybe her husband was weak or wicked or angry or vengeful.

But they did not deserve this. She had not deserved this. Her death could not be allowed to be the end of it.

And so,

When he reached home, he took a knife and cut up his concubine, limb by limb, into twelve parts and sent them into all the areas of Israel. Everyone who saw it was saying to one

another, 'Such a thing has never been seen or done, not since the day the Israelites came up out of Egypt. Just imagine! We must do something! So speak up!'
(Judges 19:29–30)

The Israelites do more than speak up. They take action. The kind of action that involved four hundred thousand armed men wielding swords (Judges 20:2). It's a hard battle and many Israelites die in the course of it, but Gibeah and all the towns belonging to the tribe of Benjamin are eventually destroyed.

Speak up. Speak out. Make the secret things known. Make the shameful deeds public. Make the nation see which horror they have been complicit in. Compel them to make amends. Force them to do better and to take up arms and fight.

For reflection
- What evidence do you see of the church and wider society being complicit in spiralling wickedness?
- Are there secret and shameful things that you need to make known?

Prayer
Lord God,
show us our sin and wickedness;
help us to see where we have been complicit in the sins
    of our society
and give us grace to repent.
Lord, grant us the courage to speak up
against the injustices and violence of our society,
and against the wickedness and abuse
inflicted by those who have power.
Lord, have mercy.
Amen.

19

Mara

'It is more bitter for me than for you, because the LORD's hand
·has turned against me!'
(Ruth 1:13)

Bible reading: Ruth 1:6–22

You'd be bitter, too, if you'd travelled with your husband to another
country and you'd arrived safely to find plenty of food and wives for
the boys but, despite all that, they'd died. All of them. Elimelek, your
husband, and Mahlon and Kilion, your sons.

You'd be bitter, too, if you'd found yourself alone and unprotected,
many miles away from home. And then you'd heard that, after all
that, the Israelites had survived the famine anyway. They had enough
food and you need never have come.

You'd be bitter, too if you'd realized that you were too old for
anyone to want you as his wife now. Too old to have more children – more sons – of your own. And though your sons had both
married, neither of them had children to bear their name and to
carry on the family.

You'd be bitter if you'd known the Lord's hand had turned against
you.

And when your daughters-in-law protested that they wanted
to come with you and that they were still your family, you'd be bitter
at having to explain it to them:

Even if I thought there was still hope for me – even if I had a
husband tonight and then gave birth to sons – would you wait
until they grew up? Would you remain unmarried for them?

No, my daughters. It is more bitter for me than for you, because the LORD's hand has turned against me!'
(Ruth 1:12–13)

You'd be bitter, even if one of them had insisted on accompanying you all the long, weary way back to Bethlehem, where you'd arrived in husbandless, childless shame. You'd be so bitter that when the people asked, 'Can this be Naomi?' you'd spit out your reply: 'Don't call me Naomi. Call me Mara.'

Don't call me 'pleasant'. Call me 'bitter'.

You'd be sure to tell them why: 'Because the Almighty has made my life very bitter. I went away full, but the LORD has brought me back empty. Why call me Naomi? The LORD has afflicted me; the Almighty has brought misfortune upon me' (Ruth 1:20–21).

You'd be bitter because of what the Lord had done.

But maybe, bit by bit, as the Lord rebuilt your family, as he gave you a new protector, as he brought a new child to put into your arms, people would look at you and they would not say, 'Mara has a son!' Because you would not be bitter then.

They would look at you and say, 'Naomi has a son!' Because you were joyful once again.

The trick for Mara, you see, was not to let the bitterness take hold, so that Naomi could grasp the happiness when it came.

For reflection

- Do you feel bitter when you look back over your life? Are you angry with the Lord? Do you feel as though he has turned his hand against you?
- How can you stop bitterness taking hold? How can you let go of grudges? How can you learn to take hold of happiness again?

Prayer

Almighty God,
forgive us for the bitterness in our hearts,
for the times our anger has been directed at you,
for the grudges we have held
and for the way we have doubted your loving care.
Help us to forgive, as you have forgiven us.
Teach us to love with the love you have shown us.
Fill us with joy and delight in the good you have done us,
that we may live in your grace every day.
Amen.

20

Ruth

At this, she bowed down with her face to the ground. She asked him, 'Why have I found such favour in your eyes that you notice me – a foreigner?'
(Ruth 2:10)

Bible reading: Ruth 2:1–23

Sometimes things don't, after all, go from bad to worse.

Sometimes when your first husband dies, when you leave your home and your country and follow your mother-in-law down the long road to her former place, and when you arrive and have nowhere to stay and no food to eat, sometimes, people will be kind. Sometimes they will let you glean for wheat in their fields. Sometimes they will even tell their workers to make sure they leave plenty of gleanings for you to find. Sometimes, when you think you will go hungry, you will be blessed abundantly.

Sometimes you'll find a man who will protect you from other men. He will show you where you can be safe and make sure you get water to drink without risking abuse or assault. Sometimes a man will have heard your story and honour you for it. He will recognize your kindness, your loyalty and your faith, and praise God for you. Sometimes an invitation to share his lunch will just be an invitation to bread and wine, and no favours will be demanded in return. Sometimes when you think you are in danger, you will be protected by a stranger.

And sometimes, you'll do what your mother-in-law tells you and risk everything. You'll go to lie in this man's bed and ask for his protection to extend still further. You'll ask him for everything: for a home, a family, a name and a place in this foreign land. You'll ask him to spread his garment over you and he still won't take advantage.

Sometimes, even when you make yourself utterly vulnerable, kneeling at his feet, a man will show you only honour and kindness. He'll send you safely home, with a generous gift of grain. He won't be demanding a dowry; he won't reject you for your foreign heritage; he won't reprimand you for your forwardness in coming to him.

And then he'll claim you lawfully and publicly. He'll wisely deal with the nearer kinsman and then he will fold you under his wing. You and your mother-in-law will be brought into his household, under his protection, bearing his name. He will be your kinsman-redeemer.

Sometimes you'll be given a second chance: a second husband. You'll bear him a child: a son. And your son, Obed, will be the father of Jesse, the father of David.

Sometimes you'll be given a second chance, a third chance, a seventh chance or a seventy-times-seventh chance. Sometimes you'll be shown grace upon grace. Sometimes you'll be folded under the Lord's wing, brought into his household, under his protection, and bear his name. He will be your kinsman-redeemer.

Sometimes, after all, things don't go from bad to worse.

For reflection

- How have you been shown unexpected grace?
- How has the Lord shown you unexpected grace?

Prayer

Gracious Lord,
you are our redeemer and our bridegroom,
and our provider and protector.
You are our abundant source of grace,
freely forgiving again and again and again.

Ruth

May we delight in your goodness and grace today,
and in all that you have provided for us
and all from which you have protected us.
Amen.

21

Hannah

So in the course of time Hannah became pregnant and gave birth to a son. She named him Samuel, saying, 'Because I asked the Lord for him.'
(1 Samuel 1:20)

Bible reading: 1 Samuel 1:1–20

She'd wept. She'd sobbed uncontrollably from a bone-deep anguish that would not be silenced.

And out of that anguish, she'd prayed. She'd pleaded. She'd begged for a child. Just one. Not to wipe the smirk off Peninnah's face. Not to prove that she could be just as good a wife. Not because she didn't know her husband loved her.

Hannah's anguish and misery sat far deeper than any of that. It wasn't Peninnah's fault that Hannah had no child. Nor was her husband to blame. No, Hannah knew that the reason she didn't have a child was because the Lord himself had closed her womb (1 Samuel 1:5).

It was God who had chosen not to give her a child. God who is sovereign over the heavens and the earth was sovereign over Hannah's fertility too. And she knew it. She knew it as she wept and as she prayed, and so she made a vow:

LORD Almighty, if you will only look on your servant's misery and remember me, and not forget your servant but give her a son, then I will give him to the LORD for all the days of his life, and no razor will ever be used on his head.
(1 Samuel 1:11)

Hannah is miserable because the Lord has forgotten her. Not that he has forgotten her existence. She isn't reminding him that she's there, as if he were an absent-minded Victorian father who can't remember how many children he has. When Hannah pleads with the Lord to remember her, she is asking for him to remember her by showing his favour; to remember her in his kindness.

Hannah's child, when he comes – if he comes – will be a delight. New babies should always be a delight, but Hannah's child will be special. He will be beloved not only for himself, but because he will be a tangible sign of the Lord's blessing on Hannah.

And so, Hannah makes this vow. If the longed-for son arrives, if the Lord answers her prayer, she will know she has enjoyed his favour and received his blessing. And that will be enough. That is what is most precious to her. For that, she will even be willing to relinquish the child himself.

She prays, and the priest prays that the Lord will grant her prayer. She and the rest of the family worship the Lord as they have come to do at Shiloh.

And then God answers. The next time she has sex with her husband, the Lord remembers her. The Lord blesses her.

Hannah gets pregnant and gives birth to a son. The first year, when he can have been no more than three months old, she stays at home while the rest of the family make their annual pilgrimage to Shiloh. But the following year she must fulfil her vow. She finds the priest and she hands him her son, Samuel, saying, 'I prayed for this child, and the LORD has granted me what I asked of him. So now I give him to the LORD. For his whole life he shall be given over to the LORD' (1 Samuel 1:27–28).

And then she sings. The wonder is that it is not a song of lament. It is not a song of bitterness at being parted from her small son. It is not a song of anger at God for taking her child away.

It is a song of joy.

It is a song of praise.

Hannah delighted in her son, no doubt. But she delighted even more in knowing that the Lord's favour was on her.

Hannah loved her child, no doubt. But Hannah loved the Lord her God far more.

Hannah was glad to receive an answer to her prayer, no doubt. But Hannah rejoiced at being able to offer back to God the most precious thing she had.

There's no question about who came first in Hannah's life. Not her husband. Not her son. But the one of whom she said, 'there is no one besides you; there is no Rock like our God' (1 Samuel 2:2).

For reflection

- What evidence is there of God's favour and blessing in your life?
- Is there a limit to what you would relinquish for the Lord's sake?

Prayer

Lord God, look on me, your servant, with favour
and remember me in your mercy.
Make me like Hannah, generous in pouring back everything
    I have received
in worship, sacrifice and praise to you,
my Saviour and my Lord.
Amen.

22

Michal

As the ark of the LORD was entering the City of David, Michal daughter of Saul watched from a window. And when she saw King David leaping and dancing before the LORD, she despised him in her heart.

(2 Samuel 6:16)

Bible reading: 2 Samuel 6:16–23

She used to love him . . . once. Back when he was young and handsome. Back when he was the nation's hero, having slung his stone at the giant Philistine warrior.

She was a bit star-struck, perhaps, when he first came to live with her family. Not just a war hero, but a poet and a musician. All the girls swooned a little bit when he was around.

She'd heard that her father planned to marry him to Merab, her elder sister, only he had turned the offer down. And then there was suddenly an opening. A possibility. A moment for the younger sister to shine and she grabbed it with both hands, never stopping to think about why her father looked so pleased or why her husband had been so willing to destroy a Philistine army to win her (1 Samuel 18:18–21).

Because, back then, all she could think about was the man she hero-worshipped. The man she loved.

Back then, Michal hadn't known her father hated him. She hadn't known Saul was plotting to kill him. She had no idea that she was just a pawn in her father's political scheming. She hadn't realized that she was supposed to hand her husband over to his death (1 Samuel 19:8–17). She hadn't known that when her husband was forced to flee for his life, her father would simply arrange another marriage for her (1 Samuel 25:44). She hadn't thought that just when she was getting what she wanted, it would be snatched away from her so swiftly.

And nor did she realize that, while she was rebuilding her life quietly with her second husband, her first was still determined to do right by his commitment to her. David had not forgotten Michal in all the years of battle and exile. And so, when the time came for David to establish himself as the new king over Israel, he also sent for his first wife to be brought to stand at his side.

Michal didn't love David any more. She was disillusioned by the way she'd been used as a political tool by her father. She had been abandoned by her husband, only to be reclaimed by him, many years later, as if she were a piece of lost property. It's not surprising that Michal had lost all her teenage passion.

It's not surprising that, as Michal watched the ark of the covenant being brought into the city of Jerusalem and 'saw King David leaping and dancing before the LORD, she despised him in her heart' (2 Samuel 6:16).

After all, David was the great and mighty king of Israel who had destroyed her father, threatened to kill her, forcibly removed her from a loving husband and now made her part of his royal harem of wives.

But, after all, David was the great and mighty king of Israel who worshipped the Lord, fulfilled the covenant promise made to his first wife, and repented humbly and deeply of his sin.

Perhaps it's not surprising that Michal despised him. But it is sad that Michal was not able to forgive him. It is sad that she did not let go of her anger and hurt. It is sad that she was not willing to reconcile with her husband.

Michal chose to despise David, but David chose to worship the Lord.

Michal ended her days childless, but David's kingdom was to endure for ever.

For reflection

- Have you ever felt used by people you had trusted? How can you recover from that?
- Why is forgiveness such an essential Christian virtue?

Prayer

Father God,
when we are the victims of hypocrisy,
when we are used by people we have trusted,
when we are shamed and mistreated by those who should
    have cared for us,
when we have come to despise those in authority over us
and when we have been abused in our own families,
give us grace
to keep trusting in you,
to keep loving you,
and to find safety and hope in you.
Amen.

23

Abigail

David said to Abigail, 'Praise be to the LORD, the God of Israel, who has sent you today to meet me. May you be blessed for your good judgment and for keeping me from bloodshed this day and from avenging myself with my own hands.'
(1 Samuel 25:32–33)

Bible reading: 1 Samuel 25:1–42

The first thing we're told about Abigail is that she is both intelligent and beautiful. Which is nice, because usually it seems as if the first thing we're told about women in the Old Testament is that they're infertile, or jealous, or wicked. But, sadly for Abigail, the second thing we're told is that her husband is surly and mean in his dealings. And like so many women in similar situations, she has turned her intelligence to handling her abusive husband. She has worked out how to manage him and how to minimize the damage he can do. It's no life, but it's Abigail's life and she's living it as best she can.

When David sends word to Nabal, asking for a favour, in return for the good treatment David had shown Nabal's men, it's no surprise that the unpleasant, ungenerous Nabal refuses. But the servant who heard the message being delivered realizes it would be worth telling Abigail about it. For, if nothing is done, 'disaster is hanging over our master and his whole household. He is such a wicked man that no one can talk to him' (1 Samuel 25:17).

Abigail thinks fast and acts fast. She gathers the provisions David had asked for and rides out to meet him. She tells him not to pay any attention to her husband and, instead, offers her gift generously.

For Abigail, it seems, recognizes in David the one who is fighting for the Lord. She asks that when he is king, he will remember her. Perhaps she even hopes that he might rescue her from her unhappy marriage. At the very least, surely she hopes for some return of the favour she has shown him.

But in the end, she does the right thing because it's the right thing. She does the right thing because she fears God more than she fears any person, even her own husband. She does the right thing because she recognizes David as the Lord's anointed servant and leader over Israel.

She can't have known that just ten days later Nabal would get blind drunk. Or that the next day, when he'd sobered up, she'd finally pluck up the courage to tell him what she had done. Or that when he heard, his heart, weakened from years of drunkenness and indulgence, would just stop. Dead.

It would have been impossible for Abigail to predict that David, when he heard of Nabal's death, would send for her and make her his wife.

Abigail fears the Lord and acts accordingly. God honours Abigail's actions and rescues her from her miserable marriage. She becomes David's wife.

But, as we're told, David already has one wife, Ahinoam, living with him in his camp, and another, Michal, currently in the household of another man.

Marriage to David was not always a bed of roses either. But I daresay Abigail, with all her intelligence, learned how to handle her second husband just as she did her first.

And I am certain that Abigail, with all her courageous faith, made a habit of doing the right thing, no matter what.

For reflection

- What should a faithful Christian woman do if she were to find herself married to a man like Nabal?

- When is it hard to do the right thing? Why should you do it anyway?

Prayer

Sovereign God,
give us the courage to face what is before us
and the faith to do what is right,
no matter where it may lead.
Teach us how to live wisely,
to love generously
and act justly
in every circumstance.
Amen.

24

Bathsheba

When Bathsheba went to King Solomon to speak to him for
Adonijah, the king stood up to meet her, bowed down to her
and sat down on his throne. He had a throne brought for the
king's mother, and she sat down at his right hand.
(1 Kings 2:19)

Bible reading: 1 Kings 2:13–25

We come, inevitably, to the one wife of David we've all heard
about. We couldn't quite have done the whole series of forty women
on David's wives, but there were many more than most people
realize. He had at least eight – Michal, Ahinoam, Abigail, Maakah,
Haggith, Abital, Eglah and Bathsheba – plus some uncounted
concubines. I expect it tells us everything we need to know that
most of these women are named only in a list of David's sons
and their mothers (1 Chronicles 3:1–9). Michal does not appear in
that list, since she had no sons and there may well have been other
wives in her position too: those who never made it into any written
list.

David's household was obviously nothing when compared with
his son Solomon's 300 wives and 700 concubines, but he still had
rather more wives than most. And, of course, more than God intends
and the Bible instructs.

So, no, it's not 'Some Enchanted Evening' when David sees Bathsheba taking a bath from the roof of his house one night and decides
he'll add her to the roster. It's not some grand romantic gesture when
David commands this woman he's never met to come to his home,
forces her into his bed, and tries to get the resulting pregnancy

passed off as her husband's. It's rape. Whether or not there was physical violence, there can have been no meaningful consent.

This isn't romance. It's just another tawdry tale of a man unwilling to control lust and unable to be satisfied with what he already has in the quest for something new. It's a seedy tale that turns to murder, when David arranges for Bathsheba's first husband to be killed in the front line of battle.

Even though David is brought to recognize his sin and repent of it, that's the kind of thing which tends to sour a relationship going forward. Which makes it all the more astonishing, when David is old and dying, that it's Bathsheba, of all his wives, who still has the ear of the king. She has the status of any royal wife, and she has the power to influence both her husband and her son.

Bathsheba is at least as badly sinned against as Michal. But Bathsheba seems to have found a way to forgive her husband. She has built a relationship of trust and respect with him.

Bathsheba has another son, after her first dies in infancy. Bathsheba's son is Solomon.

Solomon is not David's eldest son, and nor was Bathsheba David's first wife. But Solomon is the one to whom God's promises were made. And it's Bathsheba who is sent to David to remind him of those promises and ensure that Solomon inherits his father's throne (1 Kings 1).

She has the ear of the new king too. Bathsheba is welcomed into Solomon's throne room. The king bows to her and seats her at his right hand, in the place of highest honour. Perhaps partly because Solomon knows he owes his undisputed crown to his mother's intervention on his behalf, he will not refuse any request she makes (1 Kings 2:20).

It's just a shame that the request she makes on this occasion isn't hers. The usurper Adonijah isn't afraid to try to use her influence for his own ends, and it's he who sends Bathsheba to intercede for him. It backfires, of course. Perhaps if he'd disappeared quietly, Adonijah might have been forgotten. But the request he sends via Bathsheba makes Solomon see what a threat he continues to be. Adonijah does not live to see another day.

And Bathsheba fades into obscurity.

When the author of 1 and 2 Chronicles later comes to write his history of Israel, there's no mention of Bathsheba's first marriage or the vile way in which she came to be David's wife. There's nothing of her wise intervention on Solomon's behalf or her foolish intervention on Adonijah's. There is just one brief word: 'David reigned in Jerusalem for thirty-three years, and these were the children born to him there: Shammua, Shobab, Nathan and Solomon. These four were by Bathsheba, daughter of Ammiel' (1 Chronicles 3:4–5). There's nothing here that could cast a shadow on the golden reputation of the great King Solomon. Nothing to remind us that his father was an adulterer, a rapist and a murderer. Nothing to remind us of what his mother suffered at the hands of his father. Because the Bible tells a story very differently from the modern world. The Bible tells a story of redemption, a story of repentance and a story of restoration. The Bible tells a story in which even the greatest sinner can be redeemed. A story in which God's people are flawed, weak, wicked and sinful but who, in God's hands, can become great and mighty kings.

Inside every great hero of the faith beats a wicked, sinful heart and a Spirit-filled new life.

God can forgive, redeem and restore men like David.

Bathsheba could forgive a husband like David.

Could you?

For reflection

- How do you consider Christian leaders of the past?
  Are they great heroes of the faith?
- Why is it important to recognize their sins and failings as well?

Prayer

Father God,
you know the depths of sin in our hearts
and the reality of sin in our actions,
and yet, in Christ, you not only forgive us
but restore us and, by your Spirit, renew us
so that we may live in faithful obedience.
Knowing that we are forgiven sinners,
make us swift to forgive others,
to restore broken relationships
and to renew our hope in you.
Amen.

25

Tamar

And Tamar lived in her brother Absalom's house, a desolate
woman.
(2 Samuel 13:20)

Bible reading: 2 Samuel 13:1–22

Tamar seems to be having a minor renaissance as a girl's name.
I always wonder whether parents are naming their daughters after
the Tamar we've already met, whose first two husbands died; the
one who was thrown out of the family and then had to pretend to
be a prostitute to get her father-in-law to have sex with her so she
could get pregnant. Or perhaps they have in mind the Tamar we're
looking at today, whose rape by her half-brother prompted a civil
war.

Well, maybe those parents just went to Devon or Cornwall for
their holiday one year (for those of you somewhat puzzled, the River
Tamar forms most of the boundary between the two counties).

David, you remember, had at least eight wives and an unspecified
number of concubines. Unsurprisingly, therefore, he had a substan-
tial number of children. Nineteen sons by his wives and more by his
concubines. 'And Tamar was their sister' (1 Chronicles 3:9). So that
must have been fun.

Amnon was the eldest child. And he'd grown up watching his
father take wife after wife and concubine after concubine. He'd seen
the king's attitude to women: if there was one he wanted, he had her.
Like father, it turns out, like son.

Because Amnon had seen a woman he wanted. A woman he
became so obsessed with he made himself ill. And yes, there was a

part of him at least that knew he couldn't have her. Shouldn't have her. She was young. She was a virgin. And she was his sister.

Half-sister. As if that made a difference.

Amnon shouldn't have wanted Tamar, but he did. And so he was going to have her.

He gets advice from his cousin and he lays his plans. He pretends to be ill and asks for Tamar to bring him special food. And when she comes, he grabs her and tells her to come to bed with him.

Horrified, Tamar resists. This is her brother. Her *brother*.

But it's not just the wickedness of the incest that Tamar fears; she's also rightly concerned for her whole future. She would be disgraced. She couldn't marry Amnon, and there would be no hope of any kind of future for her if she were to let Amnon have his way. No one else would marry her either.

'But he refused to listen to her, and since he was stronger than she, he raped her' (2 Samuel 13:14).

And then. Well, then, Amnon's obsession takes a twist. Where he thought there was love, there is now hate. Amnon, it turns out, is the original incel.[1] He's persuaded himself he deserved this woman and that he has the right to have sex with her. And then, having done it, when he ought to despise himself, he despises her. He spits her out, ruined. Destroyed.

For Tamar, this isn't just about adding insult to injury. Her worst fears have come to pass. Amnon won't marry her. He won't give her his protection and his name. Wrong though that might have been, given their close relationship, at least it would have given Tamar a name. A place. A family.

As it is, in her grief, she goes to her brother Absalom, who gives her refuge.

---

1   An abbreviation of 'involuntary celibate'. Incels are men who blame women for their lack of sexual intimacy and sometimes condone rape as a way for men to exercise their right to sex.

'And Tamar lived in her brother Absalom's house, a desolate woman' (2 Samuel 13:20).

For reflection

- How can we prevent modern-day Amnons from treating women the way Tamar was treated?
- What refuge can we offer to modern-day Tamars in their grief and desolation?

Prayer

Dear Lord,
our hearts grieve as we see so many women like Tamar
destroyed by so many men like Amnon
in the world today.
Heal the hearts, minds and bodies
of every victim of sexual violence.
We repent of our own participation in the culture
that perpetuates such violence.
May we always be those who offer refuge
and tender kindness to those whose lives have been devastated
at the whim of others.
In Christ's name.
Amen.

26

The widow of Zarephath

'I am gathering a few sticks to take home and make a meal for myself and my son, that we may eat it – and die.'
(1 Kings 17:12)

Bible reading: 1 Kings 17:7–16

You reached the end of your tether some days ago. Now you've entered the final stages of grim acceptance. Not just for yourself. No, that would be too easy. You've had to come to terms with it for your boy as well.

Had his father lived, it would not have come to this. You're certain he would have found a way to keep you both fed, housed and warm. But it's just you now; on your own.

And it has not rained.

For years, it has not rained.

Nothing has grown worth harvesting. You've been eking out your stores, gleaning what you can find and hoping against hope for a miracle. But now, you've had to admit, you've reached the end. There isn't any more to glean. There isn't anything left to hope for.

But if it's the end, you'll go out as well as you can possibly manage.

So you're gathering sticks one last time, to make one last fire. You'll take the last grains of flour and the last drop of oil to make one last round of bread. With that, you'll take your son and you'll hold him tight in your arms and sing him to sleep. And you'll pray that he never wakes again. Because the miracle isn't coming.

And then it comes. Only, to take hold of it, you have to let go of what you have.

The prophet is asking you to make that last round of bread and give it to him. He says that you can go and make more afterwards. Is he crazy? Doesn't he understand? There is no more. There's barely enough for one portion. Not enough to share.

But he carries on, 'For this is what the LORD, the God of Israel, says: "The jar of flour will not be used up and the jug of oil will not run dry until the day the LORD sends rain on the land"' (1 Kings 17:14–15).

It sounds like a miracle. It sounds too good to be true. Make one round of bread for the prophet and never be hungry again? You look doubtfully at the last scoop of flour and the final drop of oil. Can you really give away the little you've got?

But then you look at the prophet. You listen to the promise he makes. The promise the Lord is making through him. And you think again.

What have you got to lose after all?

What use is it holding on to that last handful of flour and drop of oil?

What use holding on to what you have, if it's stopping you gaining far more than you'd ever imagined? A bottomless jar of flour, an endless flow of oil and a feast every day until the rains come.

Why wouldn't you hand over the little that you have in faith that the Lord, the God of Israel, will provide everything that you need?

For reflection

- What are you holding on to that might be stopping you from receiving the Lord's blessing in abundance?
- Which promises from God do you need to have more faith in?

Prayer

Almighty God,
show us where we are clinging too hard to the things of this world;
teach us not to be afraid to trust that you will keep your promises;
give us more faith in your loving care for us and for our loved ones;
bless us with your abundant provision for all our needs.
Amen.

27

Jezebel

'On the plot of ground at Jezreel dogs will devour Jezebel's flesh. Jezebel's body will be like dung on the ground in the plot at Jezreel, so that no one will be able to say, "This is Jezebel."'
(2 Kings 9:36–37)

Bible reading: 1 Kings 21:1–16

I wonder what you've made of the twenty-seven women we've looked at so far. I wonder if you've been surprised by how complicated some of their stories are. Have you been shocked to discover that even those women held up as models of faith in the New Testament were also jealous, angry sinners? Have you noticed how even some of those we might have assumed were on the outside of God's covenant blessings – the foreigner or the prostitute, say – turned out to be key players in God's covenant purposes?

It's almost as if these women were people.

So what about this woman? What about Jezebel, whose very name, many thousands of years later, continues to be a term of derision for a certain kind of woman. A Jezebel is shameless. Sexually shameless. Her name is given to any woman who uses her sexuality to exert power and influence.

Jezebel was shameless. And she did want power. And she was prepared to be ruthless in exercising it.

Jezebel made it her business to see that all the prophets of Yahweh were destroyed, while the prophets of the false gods were invited to eat at her table (1 Kings 18:3–4, 18–19).

Jezebel threatened to kill Elijah after his great demonstration of Yahweh's power and superiority over all the Baals – the false gods that she had taught her husband to worship (1 Kings 16:31–32; 19:2).

And when her husband was sulking because he could not have something he wanted, Jezebel was willing to get it for him by falsely accusing an innocent man and causing him to be stoned to death (1 Kings 21:1–16).

Her influence extended not only to her husband, Ahab, king of Israel (the northern kingdom), but after him to her son, Joram, and even to their son-in-law, Jehoram, king of Judah (the southern kingdom),[1] and to the next generation after them. It was only when Jehu, a new leader of a new dynasty, was anointed, that the cycle was finally broken:

> This is what the LORD, the God of Israel, says: 'I anoint you king over the LORD's people Israel. You are to destroy the house of Ahab your master, and I will avenge the blood of my servants the prophets and the blood of all the LORD's servants shed by Jezebel. The whole house of Ahab will perish. I will cut off from Ahab every last male in Israel – slave or free. I will make the house of Ahab like the house of Jeroboam son of Nebat and like the house of Baasha son of Ahijah. As for Jezebel, dogs will devour her on the plot of ground at Jezreel, and no one will bury her.
>
> (2 Kings 9:6–10)

Jezebel was wicked. There is no question about that. She was wicked, shameless, ruthless. She was promiscuous, manipulative and blood thirsty. She was idolatrous and faithless.

But she was not those things because she was a woman.

---

1 After the death of King Solomon, the son of King David, Israel split into two kingdoms. The northern kingdom of Israel was ruled by usurpers while Judah, the southern kingdom, was still ruled by David's descendants.

She was not those things because she was a woman who wore make-up and tight-fitting clothes.

She was not those things because she had breasts and hips, and was a sexual being.

Be very careful whom you call a Jezebel. Be clear about what you are calling down on her head. It's not a fate to wish on someone lightly.

For reflection

- Jezebel's sins included idolatry, ruthlessness, false accusations and murder. Who are Jezebel's heirs in today's world?
- Why is Jezebel remembered differently from her husband? Do you think women are judged more harshly than men for similar actions?

Prayer

Almighty God,
spare us from the sins of Jezebel:
may we only worship the true and living God;
may we always act with gentleness and mercy;
may we never accuse others falsely;
may we never seek the harm of others
with our hands or in our hearts.
Amen.

28

Athaliah

When Athaliah the mother of Ahaziah saw that her son was dead, she proceeded to destroy the whole royal family.
(2 Kings 11:1)

Bible reading: 2 Kings 11:1–3; 13–20

Athaliah had royal blood running in her veins. Her grandfather had been king in Israel. Her son was king in Judah. She had been a queen consort and a queen mother. And, now, there was no king left. Only children, far too young to rule the country. Athaliah would have been an excellent regent, ruling in her grandson's stead until he was old enough to do so in his own right.

But that wasn't what Athaliah wanted. That wasn't what she deserved. This was her moment.

Why should she not be queen? She was the most experienced, the most qualified and the best suited.

Why should she not trample over those who stood in her way?

Her grandchildren, that is to say. Her own grandchildren, who you might think ought to have been delighted in and played with and perhaps even a little spoiled by their doting grandmother.

But no. This was no doting grandmother. This was a murdering grandmother.

For six years Athaliah clung on to power. It can't have been easy. Any number of people must have had their eye on her throne. But then, I daresay she had something of a reputation for cold-blooded ruthlessness, given how she'd killed her way to the throne.

Whatever her reputation, it clearly did not inspire deep loyalty in her people. When the moment finally came for the true king to take his place, all Athaliah's shouts of 'Treason!' and her histrionic ripping of her clothes did not inspire one person to stand up in her defence. Not one person tried to argue her case. No one stepped forward to protect her from being taken and executed.

Athaliah chose to live by the sword and so Athaliah died by the sword: 'All the people of the land rejoiced, and the city was calm, because Athaliah had been slain with the sword at the palace' (2 Kings 11:20).

It never had to be that way. Her grandson was just a year old when his father died. Athaliah could have ruled the nation on his behalf. She could have had power. She could have had the strongest influence over Judah's next ruler. But she was greedy. She wanted it all.

And then she lost it all.

For reflection

- Why do we find Athaliah's actions so shocking? Do you think it seems worse because she was a woman?
- Are there areas in your life where you are greedy for more? When are you tempted to ride roughshod over other people to get what you want?

Prayer

Father God,
may we never be tempted to the sins of Athaliah:
to the sin of greed that always wants more;
to the sin of selfishness that is not willing to serve others;
to the sin that desires power at the expense of others;
to the sin of destroying those whom we should help to flourish;
to the sin of ruthlessness without compassion.
Father, forgive us for these sins;
forgive us and give us grace, by your Spirit,
to live with contentment, compassion and generosity.
Amen.

29

Jehosheba

> But Jehosheba, the daughter of King Jehoram and sister of
> Ahaziah, took Joash son of Ahaziah and stole him away from
> among the royal princes, who were about to be murdered.
> (2 Kings 11:2)

Bible reading: 2 Kings 11:1–12

The history of Athaliah made for pretty grim reading, but tied up in those same events was another woman. A very different woman. While Athaliah was busily murdering all the grandchildren that she could lay her hands on, Jehosheba was quietly saving the life of one of them.

Jehosheba was the daughter of a king and the sister of a king, which made her the aunt of Athaliah's grandchildren. She clearly knew what sort of woman her mother was (or possibly her stepmother; it's not clear which). When Jehosheba saw what was happening she acted, and fast:

> But Jehosheba, the daughter of King Jehoram and sister of
> Ahaziah, took Joash son of Ahaziah and stole him away from
> among the royal princes, who were about to be murdered. She
> put him and his nurse in a bedroom to hide him from Athaliah;
> so he was not killed. He remained hidden with his nurse at the
> temple of the LORD for six years while Athaliah ruled the land.
> (2 Kings 11:2–3)

The child was just a year old. He was not, of course, the first baby boy in the Bible who needed to be hidden for his life to be saved; nor would he be the last. But he was the one who was hidden for the longest. There was no way he could stay in the palace for the next six years and expect to escape his grandmother's notice. So Jehosheba arranged for him to be smuggled out to the one place even Athaliah could not go: the temple.

Jehosheba, unlike the women who had saved Moses' life many hundreds of years earlier, knew that she was doing more than protecting a baby. She knew that Athaliah was not the rightful ruler of the kingdom of Judah. She knew that God had made promises to David's descendants that should pass to her nephew. She knew that Joash was God's anointed king. And so, even though she couldn't save all the children, she saved the one on whom God's promises rested.

Joash wasn't absolutely the best king that Judah ever had, but he was better than most, and infinitely better than Athaliah. At seven years old, he took the throne, and under the guidance of the high priest who had hidden and protected him since he was a baby, he 'did what was right in the eyes of the LORD' (2 Kings 12:2).

One day, many hundreds of years later, another woman would hide a baby from a murderous ruler. That baby would also be God's anointed king, the heir to the promises that God had made to David and his descendants. That woman would not be able to save all the children from death either, but she too would save the one whom God would use to save his people. And he too would do what was right in the eyes of the Lord.

Thank God for women like that.

For reflection

- Why are there so many stories in the Bible about attacks on very young children and about the women who save some of them?
- We don't know very much about Jehosheba and her life other than this one act. What does it tell us about her and her faith?

Prayer

Almighty God,

grant us the patience to serve you quietly day by day,

to be faithful in prayer each day,

to know you from your word,

to gather with your people

and to grow in our faith,

so that in moments of crisis,

when there is no time to pause and consider,

we may act with courage,

trusting in your faithfulness to your promises,

and your sovereignty in all things.

Amen.

30

Huldah

She said to them, 'This is what the LORD, the God of Israel, says: tell the man who sent you to me, "This is what the LORD says: I am going to bring disaster on this place and its people, according to everything written in the book the king of Judah has read."'
(2 Kings 22:15–16)

Bible reading: 2 Kings 22:8–20

Prophets don't just predict the future. In fact, prophets rarely predict the future. Prophets are not fortune-tellers.

Huldah was not a fortune-teller, looking into a crystal ball to predict the future for the nation of Judah. Huldah was a prophet, as all the other Old Testament prophets, who spoke God's word into their particular historical contexts.

Sometimes prophecies aren't about the future at all but merely God's comment on past or present situations. Even when prophecies do speak about the future, they are not always promises of what *will* happen. Sometimes they are warnings of what *might* happen. Sometimes they are absolute: 'This will happen.' Often they are conditional: '*If* you continue in your ways, this will happen.'

In Huldah's day, Judah's young King Josiah sent word to tell the high priest to use the tithes appropriately for the rebuilding of the temple. For years, the temple had been allowed to fall into disrepair and the kings had not enabled true worship of the Lord to continue. But Josiah wanted to set that right. And while the temple was being repaired, the high priest rediscovered the book of the law, which had apparently lain lost and forgotten for generations.

When the book was read out to the king, he tore his clothes as a sign of repentance and told his advisors:

> Go and enquire of the LORD for me and for the people and for all Judah about what is written in this book that has been found. Great is the LORD's anger that burns against us because those who have gone before us have not obeyed the words of this book; they have not acted in accordance with all that is written there concerning us.
>
> (2 Kings 22:13)

How do you enquire of the Lord? You ask a prophet. That's what prophets do: they tell you what God says.

In this case, the prophet they ask happens to be a female prophet. They ask the wife of Shallum, who is the son of Tikvah, who is the son of Harhas, who is keeper of the wardrobe. They ask Huldah.

Huldah listens. She hears the news that the book of the law has been found and about the king's reaction to it.

And then she speaks God's word. Her prophecy is a word of warning and of promise. The warning is of God's wrath and judgment on the people who have forsaken the Lord and worshipped other gods. The promise is for King Josiah who, because of his penitence, will escape that judgment. How? By being gathered to the Lord before the destruction comes: 'Therefore I will gather you to your ancestors, and you will be buried in peace. Your eyes will not see all the disaster I am going to bring on this place' (2 Kings 2:20).

His death will be his salvation.

Death is very near at the moment I am writing this. The COVID-19 pandemic was just beginning in March 2020 when I first wrote this reflection and it is still continuing in 2021 as I am revising it. Every day, more and more people are dying after contracting this virus. Ten friends and family members of mine have died in the past year.

Death is real and it seems very frightening. But the word of God, spoken through the prophet Huldah, tells us that God's unquenchable wrath is more frightening by far. Do not fear being gathered to your grave in peace by the Lord. Fear the destruction that God will bring on those who have turned away from him.

And let your fear move you to repentance, while it is not too late.

For reflection

- Why should we fear death? How should we act on that fear?
- Why shouldn't we fear death? How can we hold on to God's promises and hope?

Prayer

Holy God,
whose anger burns against wickedness,
we come to you in repentance and grief for our own sin,
but we do not come in fear,
for you are a God of grace and mercy;
you are the source of resurrection and life.
We praise you because, in Christ, we have a sure and certain hope
for this life and the life to come.
Amen.

31
Vashti

'For the queen's conduct will become known to all the women, and so they will despise their husbands and say, "King Xerxes commanded Queen Vashti to be brought before him, but she would not come."'

(Esther 1:17)

Bible reading: Esther 1:1–22

It's been quite a party, all told. Six months' worth of pomp and ceremony celebrating the wealth and vastness of the Persian Empire, contained in all 127 of its provinces, stretching from India to Ethiopia, culminating in seven days of solid feasting in Susa, the capital city. Xerxes is showing off, big style.

Because he is the most successful person to be the king of the biggest empire. He's made the empire great again. No one's ever been more successful than he has. He's showing off his huge finances. He's making sure they all know that his IQ is one of the highest – they don't need to feel stupid or insecure; it's not their fault that they can't be as great as he is. Some people would say he's very, very, very intelligent.

And he will be phenomenal to the women. I mean, he wants to help women. Of course, they all flirt with him   consciously or unconsciously. That's to be expected. And you know, when guys tell him they want women of substance, not beautiful models, it just means they can't get beautiful models. Xerxes can get the beautiful models.

He's a winner, for sure.

It must be fabulous being married to a man like that.

While he's having his feast for a week, his wife is hosting her own banquet for the women. But Xerxes is showing off. He wants to show everyone that he can get the beautiful models. So,

> On the seventh day, when King Xerxes was in high spirits from wine, he commanded the seven eunuchs who served him – Mehuman, Biztha, Harbona, Bigtha, Abagtha, Zethar and Karkas – to bring before him Queen Vashti, wearing her royal crown, in order to display her beauty to the people and nobles, for she was lovely to look at.
> (Esther 1:10–11)

Just what any woman would want: to be paraded in front of a hall full of drunken men, with your own drunken husband grabbing you by the pussy.

Vashti does the unthinkable.

Vashti says no.

Vashti knew her husband well enough to know what would happen, no doubt: 'But when the attendants delivered the king's command, Queen Vashti refused to come. Then the king became furious and burned with anger' (Esther 1:12).

Let us be clear: if a woman cannot refuse her husband without provoking him to fury, that woman is in an abusive marriage.

Xerxes is so enraged that he has Vashti dismissed from the palace and stripped of her royal status. Even more than that, a decree is issued ensuring that all women across the empire are compelled to obey their husbands. Every man is to be master in his own household. They are afraid that other women will follow Vashti's example because the royal household is the model for all households.

This isn't the godly, sacrificial leadership of a husband for his wife, or godly sacrificial submission of a wife for her husband. This is not, to be clear, simply a complementarian view of marriage.

This is a licence for domestic abuse.

It matters who our leaders are and it matters how they conduct their personal lives. It matters that they are people of good character, not only good policy. Modern politicians may not literally be emperors but, nonetheless, they have influence through their example, as well as through their policy-making. The way they live their lives will influence the way they lead their people.

Let us be careful whom we choose to be our exemplars. Let us be careful whom we choose to be our leaders.

For reflection

- Why does the character and personal life of a political leader matter?
- Why does the character and personal life of a church leader matter?

Prayer

Father God,
we pray today for all women and men caught in abusive marriages:
give them courage and strength;
give them friends who can offer help and support;
give them a way out.
Lord, we pray for all our leaders
to have integrity and compassion,
and to have humility and good character
in their personal lives and in their public service.
In your mercy.
Amen.

32

Esther

This young woman, who was also known as Esther, had a lovely figure and was beautiful.
(Esther 2:7)

Bible reading: Esther 2:1–18

God loves beauty. God has, after all, made everything beautiful in its time (Ecclesiastes 3:11). He's made beautiful sunsets and beautiful mathematics and beautiful music. He loves to look on his beautiful creation, which reflects his own beauty.

God has made beautiful people. And, let me be clear, not just people with the inner beauty of a gentle and quiet spirit, though that is beautiful too. He's made people with beautiful eyes and beautiful hair, and with beautiful smiles and beautiful figures. That outer beauty is not something to be sneered at or disdained. It's something to be delighted in and celebrated by us, just as it is by God.

God made Esther very beautiful indeed: 'This young woman, who was also known as Esther, had a lovely figure and was beautiful' (Esther 2:7). She was beautiful enough to win the Miss Persian Empire beauty contest circa 482 BC.

She was beautiful in herself, but she also spent twelve months becoming even more beautiful: 'Before a young woman's turn came to go in to King Xerxes, she had to complete twelve months of beauty treatments prescribed for the women, six months with oil of myrrh and six with perfumes and cosmetics' (Esther 2:12). Beauty was a serious business back then, just as it is now.

God made Esther very beautiful so that she would have the opportunity to enter the palace and win the ear of the king, and thus to save the Jewish people in exile. Beauty was not the only quality that Esther needed: she showed courage, wisdom, faith and loyalty as well. But without her beauty, she would not have had the chance to show any of those other qualities.

When God made Esther 'for such a time as this', he made her beautiful enough 'for such a time as this' (Esther 4:14).

God has made you beautiful, too. You are beautiful enough for him to delight in looking on you. You are beautiful enough to be able to fulfil his plans for you.

So, celebrate your God-given beauty; delight in it. Seek an outer beauty that honours the beauty of God's glorious creation and reflects the inner beauty of your spirit, so that, both outwardly and inwardly, you will display the beauty of God himself.

For reflection

- What prompts you to delight in the beauty of God's creation?
- Do you celebrate your own God-given beauty? Do you think God delights in your outward appearance?

Prayer

Creator God,
who made everything beautiful in its time
and every person beautiful in your image,
we praise you for making us all perfectly suited
to the works you have planned for us to do.
As we rejoice and delight in the beauty of your good creation,
may we also rejoice and delight in the beauty of the people you
    have made.
As we seek the inner beauty of a godly character,
may we also celebrate the outer beauty you have given us.
Amen.

33

Gomer

'Go, show your love to your wife again, though she is loved by another man and is an adulteress.'
(Hosea 3:1)

Bible reading: Hosea 1:1–11; 3:1–5

It seemed like the full-on fairy tale. It was the *Pretty Woman* happy ending for the prostitute and the prophet when Hosea took Gomer, 'the promiscuous woman' (Hosea 1:2), and married her. They settled down. They had a family together. That should have been the happily ever after.

But, you know, that's actually the first chapter of their story, not the last.

Because change is hard. External change is the easy part: the new home, the new husband, the new children. It's internal change that's hard: the new mindset, the new patterns of thinking, the new beliefs about yourself and the world.

For Gomer, it must have been hard to believe that suddenly she was safe, secure and beloved after living in such a precarious way previously. It must have been hard to stop the habit of catching the eye of any likely bloke who wandered past. It must have been hard not to flirt with them. It must have been hard to keep working at a relationship with the same man, day after day. It must have been hard to learn how to think of herself as a mother, of having responsibility for other people.

It is hard suddenly to become a different person, with a different life.

And so, perhaps inevitably, Gomer failed. She was unfaithful to Hosea. She went off with another man.

But that's not the end of this story either.

> The LORD said to [Hosea], 'Go, show your love to your wife again, though she is loved by another man and is an adulteress. Love her as the LORD loves the Israelites, though they turn to other gods and love the sacred raisin cakes.'
> (Hosea 3:1)

God loves his bride, Israel, despite her unfaithfulness. He loves her despite her adultery in turning to false gods. He doesn't wash his hands of her and walk away, even though he has every right to. He loves her, so he goes after her. He woos her tenderly, and heals her hurts, and forgives her sins, and restores her in their marriage (Hosea 2:14–23).

Hosea is to love Gomer in the same way that the Lord loves Israel. Even though she has left him. Even though she has gone off with another man. Even though she has committed adultery, he is not to wash his hands of her and walk away. Hosea is to go after Gomer. He is to woo her, to heal her and forgive her, and restore her in their marriage.

I don't know how many times Hosea had to do that for Gomer. I don't know how many times she had to forgive him too. But I do know that this is the kind of love which lasts: the kind of love which doesn't expect or demand perfection; the kind which extends grace and forgiveness.

It is the kind of love we all, desperately, need.

For reflection

- Why is forgiveness so important in love?
- How many times has the Lord forgiven you? How many times are you willing to forgive others?

Prayer

Loving God,
we are in awe at the depth of your love,
which persists with us and pursues us,
no matter how often we turn away.
We are in awe at the depth of your grace,
which forgives us and restores us,
no matter how unfaithful we become.
Change us from the inside, Lord God,
make our hearts inclined to love you
and quick to forgive others
as you forgive us.
Amen.

34

The Shulammite

I belong to my beloved, and his desire is for me.
(Song of Songs 7:10)

Bible reading: Song of Songs 4:1–5:1

While I was working on the original blog posts that formed the basis
for this book, a couple of people asked whether it was easy to find forty
women to write about, or whether I had found myself scrambling
around to make up the numbers. To be honest, it was pretty easy.
There were quite a few women who were on an earlier version of the
list, later replaced by others I'd forgotten but knew I wanted to
include.

But there is one woman who has been on every version of the list:
the woman at the heart of the Song of Songs. The bride (Song 4:8–11).
The beautiful darling (Song 4:1). The vineyard, the garden, the
orchard of fruits (Song 4:12–14). The stately palm tree, as majestic as
armies and as lovely as Jerusalem (Song 7:8; 6:4).

She's one of just a handful of unnamed women on the list and
she's the only one who probably isn't a historical figure. She's the
Shulammite, that is, the Solomoness. She's the wise woman who
teaches the daughters of Jerusalem how to love wisely but not too
soon (Song 2:7). She's the bride of the king, brought up out of the
wilderness on the arm of her beloved (Song 8:5), who will be crowned
on his wedding day (Song 3:11).

She's not afraid to go after what she wants, even when it takes her
out into the dangers of the city streets. She's not ashamed to bring
her lover home to meet her mother. She's proud to be the one beloved

of just one man, unlike the many myriad wives and concubines of Solomon (Song 8:11–12).

She's in love, you see. She is her beloved's and he is hers. She's longing for his kisses and his embrace. Every moment apart from him is agony and every moment in his presence is deep rest.

For the first time since the curse fell on Adam and Eve, mutual desire is unencumbered with manipulative oppression. When she speaks, she no longer needs to say, 'My desire is for him but he rules over me' (see Genesis 3:16). No, this woman can say proudly, 'I am my beloved's, and his desire is for me' (Song 7:10, esv).

This is no ordinary woman and her lover is no ordinary man. Their love does not belong in a broken, barren, sinful world. Their love belongs in a sanctuary. In a garden. In a new Eden, a promised Canaan, a temple-fragranced land flowing with milk and honey. Their love belongs in a safe space, unthreatened by serpents and sin. Their love takes them back into a place where the Lord himself can walk among the trees and flowers.

This is no ordinary woman and her lover is no ordinary man. She doesn't just belong in a garden, a new Eden, a promised Canaan. She *is* the garden, the Eden, the Canaan, the promised land. She is restored, renewed, revived Israel, flourishing as the desert returning to bloom. He isn't just any bridegroom, any shepherd, any king. He is *the* bridegroom, shepherd, king who is to be worshipped like the Lord himself. He is the one who leads his bride out of the wilderness and into the promised land.

And she ends the book as she began it, longing to be with her beloved, in their paradise, for ever, with nothing to separate them.

She's still longing: 'Come away, my beloved, and be like a gazelle or like a young stag on the spice-laden mountains' (Song 8:14).

We're all still longing: 'The Spirit and the bride say, "Come!" And let the one who hears say, "Come!"'(Revelation 22:17).

Amen. Come, Lord Jesus.

For reflection

- Are you longing for the bridegroom's return? What are you most longing for about that time?
- How do your experiences of human relationships help you to understand the relationship God has with his people?

Prayer

Heavenly bridegroom,
you have demonstrated the depth of your love for us
in the extraordinary sacrifice you made for us.
As we wait for the consummation of that love,
may we live in eager anticipation,
longing to be with you,
longing to be held by you,
longing to delight in your presence
and longing for freedom from fear.
May each day of longing increase our love
and desire for you.
Come, Lord Jesus.
Amen.

35

Mary

'I am the Lord's servant,' Mary answered. 'May your word to
me be fulfilled.'
(Luke 1:38)

Bible reading: Luke 1:26–38

It's an odd thing that in modern culture, angels are usually depicted
as women – or sometimes as young children – with flowing hair and
an ethereal quality about them. Even on Christmas cards, when the
angels are definitely supposed to be biblical angels, they quite often
have more in common with school nativity plays or New Age ideas
than they do with the Bible. For a start, all the specific angels we're
told about in the Bible are male.

And almost all of them are sent to speak to men: to Abraham,
to Moses, to Balaam and to Gideon, among others. But also, you
remember, to Hagar. Even at the beginning of Luke's Gospel, the first
angel who appears is sent to Zechariah, to tell him that his wife will
bear him a son. But the second angel, the angel Gabriel, is sent to a
woman. Because, of course, Joseph's fiancée isn't going to bear him
a son. Mary will bear a son, but he will be the Son of the Most High,
and a son (descendant) of his father, King David, and he will be the
Son of God (Luke 1:32, 35).

Blimey.

Well, let's go back to the beginning. The angel starts with what
sounds like a perfectly civil greeting, telling Mary that she is highly
favoured and that the Lord is with her. But Mary is troubled. She's
not at all sure where this is going and, frankly, she's scared. Here's
the thing: the Lord doesn't just send angels to tell people that they're

doing fine. You don't get that kind of messenger just to say, 'Keep calm and carry on.' An angel generally means there's going to be trouble and you need to listen to God's plan to get you out of it. It's no surprise that the first thing angels often have to say to people is 'Don't be afraid'.

But, honestly, I'm not sure that the rest of Gabriel's message sounds all that reassuring. He tells Mary again that she has found favour with God. And then calmly carries on to say that she's going to have a son and will call him Jesus. Well, OK. She's engaged to be married. She's probably hoping that she will have a son. And Jesus – the Greek form of the old Hebrew name Joshua – is a perfectly reasonable name to give him.

Except . . . this baby will be great and will be called the Son of the Most High. He will be a king. On David's throne. He will reign over all Israel for ever.

Frankly, at the end of that, my question wouldn't be: 'How can this be, since I am a virgin?' My questions would be: 'Huh? There's already a king over there and any child of mine and Joseph's is miles away from the royal line. And, um, the Most High? How can my baby be the son of, well, God? What on earth are you talking about?'

But Mary has a point too. So the angel explains how the Holy Spirit will come over her and God's mighty power will cause her to conceive miraculously. So that her son, conceived by the Holy Spirit, will indeed be the holy one, the Son of God.

Honestly, I'd still have a ton of questions at that point. I still have a ton of questions now, and this isn't even happening to me.

Mary, however, shows just why the Lord's favour is on her and not on me. Because she hears the Lord's messenger and she believes him. She doesn't demand more explanations. She doesn't raise objections. She doesn't point out all the reasons why this makes no sense at all.

Mary trusts and obeys. 'I am the Lord's servant,' she says. 'May your word to me be fulfilled' (Luke 1:38).

This angel's visit, like so many others, is a sign that there is trouble brewing. And, as so often, it's the angel who explains how that trouble can be avoided. For this son that Mary will bear is to be called Jesus.

Jesus. Joshua. Yeshua. Saviour.

When God sends his Saviour, don't ask questions. Don't raise objections. Don't try to pick apart the logic.

When God sends his Saviour, be like Mary. Trust and obey.

For reflection

- Is Mary right to be alarmed by the angel? Do you fear what God might be demanding of your life?
- When you consider God's great salvation plan, what is your response? Do you require answers and explanations or are you willing simply to trust? Do you think we need to understand it all?

Prayer

Father God,
thank you that Mary found favour in your eyes,
that she responded to your call with obedience and faith,
and that the son you gave her was indeed the Son of God –
    the Saviour.
May we also find favour in your eyes,
that we too should be your servants,
responding to your call with obedience and faith
as we put our trust in the Son of God, our Saviour.
Amen.

36

The woman
who had been bleeding

'Daughter, your faith has healed you. Go in peace and be freed
from your suffering.'
(Mark 5:34)

Bible reading: Mark 5:24–34

Twelve years. Twelve *years* you have been bleeding. Twelve years of
debilitating weakness, pain and fear. You've done everything you
can. You've consulted every doctor you can afford. You've spent
all your money. You've spent all your hope. There's nowhere else
to turn.

Twelve years of debilitating weakness, pain, fear and shame.
Twelve years of being cut off from the community. Twelve years of
uncleanness and shame.

Did I mention the shame?

There's no shame in bleeding. There's no shame in being a woman.
It's normal. It's expected. There are rules for how to live with it: where
you can sit and where you can lie down, and how to avoid spreading
the uncleanness. And you do it every month for a few days, until your
bleeding has finished, and then you go to the priest, who makes
atonement for your uncleanness, and that's all done until the next
month (Leviticus 15:30).

There are also rules for when the bleeding continues beyond
its normal time. Rules that define you as unclean for as long as you
keep bleeding and another seven days beyond that (Leviticus
15:25, 28).

But there are no rules for when the bleeding does not stop. Ever. For twelve years you have been unclean. For twelve years you have had to separate yourself from others within your household. For twelve years your uncleanness has been contagious. Your chair, your bed – they share your uncleanness; they make other people unclean too.

How could you not feel ashamed? Your bleeding makes you unclean in ways that are public. Your bleeding marks you out. Your bleeding makes you unable to bear children. If you have a husband, your bleeding will make him unclean whenever you have sex. You can't enter the temple courts. You aren't fit to be seen in public.

But then you hear about him. The healer. The teacher. The one who made the paralysed man walk. The one who made the leper clean.

And, for the first time in years, you begin to hope again. What if he could do that for you? What if he could heal you? What if he could make you clean?

So you venture out among the crowds. You don't need to speak to him. You don't need him to stop to do anything. You just need to touch his clothes and you will be healed.

He's there. Within reach. You feel for his cloak and, in that moment, you know. The bleeding has stopped. You're free. You're free for the first time in twelve years. And you don't shout or cry or draw any attention to yourself. You just stand, silently revelling in the healing you have longed for.

But that isn't the end of it. The healer, Jesus, turns around to find you and you can't hide from him. So you walk forward and instinctively fall to your knees before him, trembling as you tell him everything.

You'd hoped for the healing but you'd never dared to dream of what comes next. He speaks, so that the crowd can hear: 'Daughter, your faith has healed you. Go in peace and be freed from your suffering.'

He's telling them as much as he's telling you. You are healed. You are free from your suffering. Free from your shame. Free indeed.

For reflection

- What shame are you holding on to? What would happen if you were to trust Jesus with that shame?
- What things are people shamed for in our society? What would happen if we were to treat those people as Jesus would?

Prayer

Lord Jesus,
thank you for the tender care you show to those who are suffering;
for the sympathy you have for those who are ashamed;
for the attention you pay to those who are overlooked;
for the love you lavish on those who are unlovely;
for the mercy you extend to all those who fall to their knees in repentance;
for the grace you pour out on all who acknowledge their weakness;
for the welcome you give to all who reach out to you.
Amen.

37

The forgiven woman

'Therefore, I tell you, her many sins have been forgiven – as her
great love has shown.'
(Luke 7:47)

Bible reading: Luke 7:36–50

It's a particular sort of privilege to know what you need. Many of
us spend our whole lives blundering around, and trying and failing
to work out what will solve our problems, make us happy and bring
us freedom. But occasionally someone is in a situation so clear and
stark that it's obvious what they need.

And occasionally that person will find it.

The paralysed man they brought to Jesus thought that he needed
physical healing more than anything. But Jesus knew he needed forgiveness for his sins.

The Pharisees who came to hear Jesus thought that they needed
to know whether Jesus was a true prophet. But Jesus knew they
needed forgiveness for their sins.

The sinful woman who came to Jesus knew that what she needed
was forgiveness for her sins. And when she came to Jesus, she
received just that.

We're not given any details about her 'sinful life', but she was
probably a prostitute or adulterer. Whatever the precise nature of
her sin, it was public and notorious. She had no illusions about it.
She wasn't deceiving herself that she was justified in what she did. She
wasn't pretending that she was keeping God's law or living according
to the standards of the Pharisees. She knew what she was and she
knew what she needed.

So when she hears about this extraordinary man who is going around healing sick people, exorcising demons and raising children from the dead, no doubt she's as curious as anyone would have been. But when she hears that this man invites tax collectors for dinner and tells them that he hasn't come to 'call the righteous but sinners to repentance' (Luke 5:32), her ears prick up. That's her.

She knows she's a sinner. And this man – this Jesus – has come to call people like her. He's offering forgiveness, just as he forgave the paralysed man – and proved it by making him walk.

So she joins the dots: she's a sinner; Jesus is calling her to repent and he's offering forgiveness. The forgiveness only God can offer. No one has ever done anything like that before.

No one could have done. She knew what she needed but, until Jesus came, she had no way of getting it. She knew her sin and she knew she needed to repent of that. To turn to God and turn from her sinful way of life. To turn to Christ for forgiveness.

There's only one way for her respond to that. She purchases an expensive jar of perfume and carries it to the place where Jesus is having dinner. On coming to stand by him, she is overcome with emotion and begins to weep. Her tears fall on his feet, so she kneels to kiss his feet, to wipe them with her own hair and then to anoint them with the perfume she has brought. It's the only way she knows to honour and worship this man who has done for her what only God can do: forgive her. It's the only way she knows to show him how much she loves him.

She knew that she needed so much forgiveness – more than any-one else she could think of. Her great love for Jesus proved how much she had been forgiven – more than anyone else she could think of.

For Jesus, this woman became the model for forgiveness, putting to shame Simon and all the other Pharisees who had failed to show Jesus the basic level of respect due to a guest. She loved him so much because she had been forgiven so much.

For reflection

- How much have you been forgiven by Christ?
- How much do you love Christ?

Prayer

Heavenly Father,
open our eyes to the depths of our sin;
teach us daily our need of a Saviour;
make us always swift to repent
and to seek the joy of forgiveness.
May we know how much we have been forgiven,
and may it be shown in our great love for Christ,
our worship and submission to him,
to his glory.
Amen.

38

The woman at the well

Many of the Samaritans from that town believed in him because
of the woman's testimony.
(John 4:39)

Bible reading: John 4:4–26, 39–42

In the Bible, it seems, women needed to watch whom they met at the
well. Very often, they ended up married as a result of these meetings:
Rebekah to Isaac, Rachel to Jacob and Zipporah to Moses (Genesis 24;
Genesis 29; Exodus 2). For Hagar, it was a different sort of man: the
Lord's messenger (Genesis 16). In Proverbs 5 and Song of Songs 4,
women *are* the well for their bridegrooms, who meet them there.

But this is Jesus. His well-meeting surely can't be the beginning
of a betrothal story, can it? This woman is not offering herself as a
well to him, is she?

He asks her for a drink. From the well, of course. Water from the
well where she is drawing water for herself at an unusual time of day,
when everyone else is safely indoors. Water from this woman who
isn't part of polite society. And even if she were, it would be polite
Samaritan society. What is this Jewish man doing, asking her for
water?

He doesn't even need the water. He's got his own special water:

Everyone who drinks this water will be thirsty again, but
whoever drinks the water I give them will never thirst. Indeed,
the water I give them will become in them a spring of water
welling up to eternal life.
(John 4:13–14)

What kind of water can this be that keeps you from ever being thirsty again? What kind of well becomes a spring welling up to eternal life?

She doesn't understand but she knows she wants it. This man isn't like all those other men women have met at the well. He isn't like all the many other men the Samaritan woman has known. This man isn't taking something from her, even if that were only water. He's inviting her to ask him for something, and what he offers is not just water.

And then he sees right inside her; straight to her identity. He sees that – like Rebekah, Rachel, Hagar and Zipporah – she isn't married. But nor is she an innocent virgin. This woman has a chequered past and a chequered present. She's lived with many men and she's been married to some of them.

This is a well-meeting like no other. It's not about sexual desire and it's not about betrothal. It's about worship and eternal life, and about identity and revelation. This man recognizes her as one who will worship him in spirit and truth, and he reveals himself as the Messiah who is to be worshipped. The Messiah, you will remember, who is the bridegroom. Perhaps this is a betrothal scene after all.

It's a well-meeting like all the others, for it is utterly life-changing and not just for this one woman. She, who has met the Messiah, the Christ, immediately goes to tell all the others in her village. They believe her, and then they meet Jesus and they believe him. The Samaritans are brought back into the kingdom, through this one woman, well-met at the well by the true bridegroom of the church.

For reflection

- What's your story of meeting Christ? Have you told people about it?
- How was meeting Christ a life-changing event for you? Can other people see that?

Prayer

Lord Jesus Christ,
thank you for meeting me.
Thank you for filling me with the life-giving water
that always satisfies
and that wells up into eternal life.
Thank you for changing me;
thank you for changing my life
and bringing me into your eternal kingdom,
and into your people, your church,
so that, together, we may become a bride fit for you,
our heavenly bridegroom.
Amen.

39

Mary and Martha

'Lord,' Martha said to Jesus, 'if you had been here, my brother
would not have died . . .'

When Mary reached the place where Jesus was and saw
him, she fell at his feet and said, 'Lord, if you had been here, my
brother would not have died.'
(John 11:21, 32)

Bible reading: John 11:17–37

Mary and Martha, along with their brother Lazarus, were among
Jesus' closest friends. They were not part of the twelve; they were not
in that inner circle of teaching and discipleship. They didn't travel
with him and they were not sent out by him. But they knew him,
loved him and welcomed him into their home. They listened to him
teach and they brought him food to eat. They were his support
bubble. They were his friends.

Some people say that men and women can't be friends. Mary,
Martha and Jesus knew otherwise. When the worst happened, when
Lazarus died, they knew that they would be there for one another.
The sisters knew that their friend would care. And they knew that he
would come.

But he had not come in time. First Martha and then Mary said
the same thing to Jesus, in grief and perhaps with a note of reproach:
'If you had been here, my brother would not have died' (John
11:21, 32).

They knew Jesus, you see. They knew who and what he was. They
knew what he could do and they knew the compassion that motivated
him to do it. They knew he had healed strangers, sinners and enemies.

Considering all that he had done for those people, how much more would he have done for his dear friend Lazarus?

But he did not come. He did not come in time for Lazarus.

And yet.

And yet, Martha and Mary do not blame Jesus for their brother's death. They don't accuse him of not caring. They don't turn their backs on him and shut him out of their grief.

Martha, dear Martha, with her firm grasp of gospel theology, knows that all hope is not lost. She knows that, even now, Jesus could act. She knows that her brother will rise again on the last day. She grieves, but she does not grieve without hope, because she knows the one who is the resurrection and the life.

Mary, sweet Mary, with her tender heart and emotional instinct, knows that Christ is her only source of comfort. She goes to him quickly out of her sorrow and falls at his feet, still weeping. She brings her tears to him; they are the only possible expression of her faith in that moment.

In their time of suffering, they send for Jesus. They trust his timing; they hold on to the hope he offers and they find in him their only source of true comfort. And more than that, they find in him the friend who cares. The friend who loves. The friend who weeps.

Jesus wept. Even knowing what he was about to do. Even knowing that Lazarus would not be long in that grave, he wept.

Because death is always devastating. Because loss and separation are always painful. Because grief is the price we pay for love.

For reflection

- What does it mean to you to have Christ as your dearly beloved friend?
- When suffering comes, where do you turn? What hope and comfort do you find in Christ?

Prayer

Lord Jesus,
we turn to you in our suffering,
knowing that you too have suffered grief and loss,
rejection and death.
We turn to you in our tears,
knowing that you are the source of all true comfort,
all hope and reconciliation.
We turn to you in faith,
knowing that you can move mountains,
heal the sick, raise the dead and redeem the sinner.
Lord Jesus, there is no one else to whom we can turn,
for you have the words of eternal life.
We turn to you.
Amen.

40

Mary Magdalene

Mary Magdalene went to the disciples with the news: 'I have seen the Lord!'
(John 20:18)

Bible reading: John 20:1–18

We began this series with a woman in a garden and so we end it with a woman in a garden. The first woman, Eve, was with her husband in the garden of Eden, where they walked freely and talked with the Lord God. This final woman, Mary Magdalene, was with a man she believed to be a gardener, until she talked with him and recognized him for who he was: the Lord.

Mary Magdalene had been present to witness Christ's death (John 19:25). She came to the tomb of his burial and saw the stone which had been rolled away (John 20:1). But still, she did not understand. She thought the body had been stolen; hidden or removed by the Roman guards or possibly the Jewish authorities. Even in death, she thought, they would not allow him to rest in peace.

She went to call the men, the disciples, who might be able to do something about it. Simon Peter came, and so did John, to examine the tomb, to see what had happened. They did not understand and they went away.

But Mary stayed. She stayed to weep. Presumably that was why she had come to the tomb in the first place, to continue the process of mourning. And though the body was not there, her grief still had to find expression. She stayed and so it was she to whom the angels spoke. She stayed and so it was she who met the gardener.

The angels and the gardener all ask her the same question: 'Woman, why are you crying?' (John 20:13, 15). It's a rhetorical question; they know why she is crying. But as she answers them, she reveals her heart to them.

'They have taken my Lord away,' she says (John 20:13). Because even though he has been crucified, died and buried, he is still her Lord. He is still her Master, her Teacher, her Christ, her Lord and her God.

'I don't know where they have put him,' she says. 'Tell me where you have put him, and I will get him' (John 20:15). Because she still wants to honour him, even in his death. She wants to ensure that he has the proper anointing, the proper burial clothes and the proper tomb. Because she needs to know where he is in order to be near him. Even though he is dead, he is still the most important person to her.

And then, with one word, Jesus turns the whole world upside down.

'Mary.'

He calls her by name. It is the first word that reveals him as the risen Christ, and it is a woman's name. By it she knows him, just as he knows her. By it he proves that he is alive, just as she is. By it he cares for her, just as she has come to his grave to care for him.

Of course she wants to cling to him. Of course she wants to touch him and hold him to her and never let him go. Of course.

But the risen Christ has a different task for her. This woman, Mary Magdalene, is to be the first witness of the new life; the first herald of the resurrection. She is the one to go to Jesus' own disciples and tell them, with eyes bright and joy bursting forth, 'I have seen the Lord!' (John 20:18).

From the first garden to this new garden.

From the first life to new life.

Women have been part of God's great story from the beginning to the very end. They are not important because they are women. They are important because they are people. God's people. Saints and sinners. Victims and heroes. Faithful and courageous. Wicked and cowardly. Caring, compassionate and kind. Brave, beautiful and bold. Ordinary and extraordinary. Women who show us the worst wickedness imaginable and women who show us the deepest faith of all.

For reflection

- Why does it matter that a woman was given this high honour of being the first to witness the resurrection?
- Consider the women in these studies and the women in your life: in your church, in your family, at your workplace, among your friends. What can you learn from these women?

Prayer

Almighty God,
thank you for all that we have learned about you and about
    ourselves
from the women whose lives are recorded in your word.
Thank you for those whose faith is an example to us
and those whose wickedness is a warning to us;
for those whose courage is an inspiration to us
and those whose compassion is a model for us.
Thank you for those you used to preserve your people
and those who spread the good news to all the nations.
Thank you for those who cared for Christ on earth
and all those who have been cared for by him.
Thank you that for as many women as there are,
there are as many ways to love, serve and follow you faithfully.
May we go and do likewise.
Amen.

Further reading

Women in the Bible

Fitzpatrick, Elyse, and Eric Schumacher, *Worthy: Celebrating the value of women* (Minneapolis, MN: Bethany House, 2020)

Nielson, Kathleen B., *Women and God: Hard questions. Beautiful truth* (Epsom: The Good Book Company, 2018)

Tidball, Derek and Dianne, *The Message of Women: Creation, grace and gender* (London: IVP, 2012)

Christian life and faith

Anderson, Hannah, *Made for More: An invitation to live in God's image* (Chicago, IL: Moody, 2014)

Anyabwile, Kristie, ed., *His Testimonies, My Heritage: Women of Color on the Word of God* (Epsom: The Good Book Company, 2019)

Dickens, Sharon, *Unexceptional: Ordinary women doing extraordinary things through God* (Leyland: 10Publishing, 2019)

Hardyman, Julian, *Jesus, Lover of My Soul: Fresh pathways to spiritual passion* (London: IVP, 2020)

Abuse

Denhollander, Rachael, *What Is a Girl Worth? My story of breaking the silence and exposing the truth about Larry Nassar and USA gymnastics* (Carol Stream, IL: Tyndale Momentum, 2019)

Greenberg, Jennifer Michelle, *Not Forsaken: A story of life after abuse – how faith brought one woman from victim to survivor* (Epsom: The Good Book Company, 2019)

Identity, shame and self

Davis Nelson, Heather, *Unashamed: Healing our brokenness and finding freedom from shame* (Wheaton, IL: Crossway Books, 2016)

Kruger, Melissa B., *The Envy of Eve: Finding contentment in a covetous world* (Fearn, Ross-shire: Christian Focus Publications, 2012)

Kruger, Melissa B., ed., *Identity Theft: Reclaiming the truth of who we are in Christ* (Deerfield, IL.: The Gospel Coalition, 2018)

Witt, Sophie de, *Compared to Her: How to experience true contentment* (Epsom: The Good Book Company, 2012)

Marriage, singleness and sex

Ash, Christopher, *Married for God: Making your marriage the best it can be* (Nottingham: IVP, 1999)

Gregoire, Sheila Wray, *The Good Girl's Guide to Great Sex: (And you thought bad girls have all the fun)* (Grand Rapids, MI: Zondervan, 2012)

Krieg, Matt and Laurie, *An Impossible Marriage: What our mixed-orientation marriage has taught us about love and the gospel* (London: IVP, 2020)

Welcher, Rachel Joy, *Talking Back to Purity Culture: Rediscovering faithful Christian sexuality* (Downers Grove, IL: IVP, 2020)

Wharton, Kate, *Single-minded: Being single, whole and living life to the full* (Oxford: Monarch, 2013)

Infertility

Ivey, Jonny and Joanna, *Silent Cries: Experiencing God's love after losing a baby* (London: IVP, 2021)

Margesson, Eleanor, and Sue McGowan, *Just the Two of Us? Help and strength in the struggle to conceive* (Nottingham: IVP, 2012)

Further reading

Wedgeworth, Abbey, *Held: 31 biblical reflections on God's comfort and care in the sorrow of miscarriage* (Epsom: The Good Book Company, 2020)

Church Society is a fellowship
contending to reform and renew
the Church of England in biblical faith.

We work prayerfully, in partnership with
others, through political engagement in the
church, and by our publishing and patronage work
to equip God's people to live God's word.

Church Society

EQUIPPING GOD'S
PEOPLE TO LIVE
GOD'S WORD

Church Society members are clergy
and lay people in the Church of England
who are engaged in parishes, in deanery
and diocesan synods, and in the national
church. Members meet regularly for
online and in-person events, pray for
each other, and enjoy fellowship together.

For more information about Church
Society and to join us, please visit

churchsociety.org